Macmillan Computer Science Series

Consulting Editor
Professor F.H. Sumner, University of Manchester

S.T. Allworth and R.N. Zobel, *Introduction to Real-time Software Design, second edition*
Ian O. Angell and Gareth Griffith, *High-resolution Computer Graphics Using FORTRAN 77*
Ian O. Angell and Gareth Griffith, *High-resolution Computer Graphics Using Pascal*
M. Azmoodeh, *Abstract Data Types and Algorithms*
C. Bamford and P. Curran, *Data Structures, Files and Databases*
Philip Barker, *Author Languages for CAL*
A.N. Barrett and A.L. Mackay, *Spatial Structure and the Microcomputer*
R.E. Berry, B.A.E. Meekings and M.D. Soren, *A Book on C, second edition*
G.M. Birtwistle, *Discrete Event Modelling on Simula*
B.G. Blundell, C.N. Daskalakis, N.A.E. Heyes and T.P. Hopkins, *An Introductory Guide to Silvar Lisco and HILO Simulators*
T.B. Boffey, *Graph Theory in Operations Research*
Richard Bornat, *Understanding and Writing Compilers*
Linda E.M. Brackenbury, *Design of VLSI Systems — A Practical Introduction*
J.K. Buckle, *Software Configuration Management*
W.D. Burnham and A.R. Hall, *Prolog Programming and Applications*
J.C. Cluley, *Interfacing to Microprocessors*
J.C. Cluley, *Introduction to Low Level Programming for Microprocessors*
Robert Cole, *Computer Communications, second edition*
Derek Coleman, *A Structured Programming Approach to Data*
Andrew J.T. Colin, *Fundamentals of Computer Science*
Andrew J.T. Colin, *Programming and Problem-solving in Algol 68*
S.M. Deen, *Fundamentals of Database Systems*
S.M. Deen, *Principles and Practice of Database Systems*
Tim Denvir, *Introduction to Discrete Mathematics for Software Engineering*
P.M. Dew and K.R. James, *Introduction to Numerical Computation in Pascal*
M.R.M Dunsmuir and G.J. Davies, *Programming the UNIX System*
D. England et al., *A Sun User's Guide*
K.C.E. Gee, *Introduction to Local Area Computer Networks*
J.B. Gosling, *Design of Arithmetic Units for Digital Computers*
M.G. Hartley, M. Healey and P.G. Depledge, *Mini and Microcomputer Systems*
Roger Hutty, *Z80 Assembly Language Programming for Students*
Roland N. Ibbett, *The Architecture of High Performance Computers*
Patrick Jaulent, *The 68000 — Hardware and Software*
P. Jaulent, L. Baticle and P. Pillot, *68020-30 Microprocessors and their Coprocessors*
J.M. King and J.P. Pardoe, *Program Design Using JSP — A Practical Introduction*
H. Kopetz, *Software Reliability*
E.V. Krishnamurthy, *Introductory Theory of Computer Science*
V.P. Lane, *Security of Computer Based Information Systems*
Graham Lee, *From Hardware to Software — an introduction to computers*
A.M. Lister, *Fundamentals of Operating Systems, third edition*
G.P. McKeown and V.J. Rayward-Smith, *Mathematics for Computing*
Brian Meek, *Fortran, PL/1 and the Algols*
A. Mével and T. Guéguen, *Smalltalk-80*
Barry Morrell and Peter Whittle, *CP/M 80 Programmer's Guide*
Derrick Morris, *System Programming Based on the PDP11*
Y. Nishinuma and R. Espesser, *UNIX — First contact*
Pim Oets, *MS-DOS and PC-DOS — A Practical Guide*
Christian Queinnec, *LISP*
E.J. Redfern, *Introduction to Pascal for Computational Mathematics*
Gordon Reece, *Microcomputer Modelling by Finite Differences*
W.P. Salman, O. Tisserand and B. Toulout, *FORTH*
L.E. Scales, *Introduction to Non-linear Optimization*
Peter S. Sell, *Expert Systems — A Practical Introduction*
Colin J. Theaker and Graham R. Brookes, *A Practical Course on Operating Systems*

Continued overleaf

D0266793

Program Design Using JSP — a Practical Introduction

M. J. King and J. P. Pardoe

Liverpool Polytechnic
Byrom Street
Liverpool L3 3AF

MACMILLAN

First published 1985
Reprinted 1986, 1987 (twice), 1988

Published by
MACMILLAN EDUCATION LTD
Houndmills, Basingstoke, Hampshire RG21 2XS
and London
Companies and representatives
throughout the world

Printed in Hong Kong

British Library Cataloguing in Publication Data
Pardoe, J.P.
Introduction to program design using JSP.
1. Structured programming
I. Title
001.64'2   QA76.6
ISBN 0-333-39535-2
ISBN 0-333-39536-0 Pbk

Contents

Preface

Aims of the book

This text aims to provide a practical course for those who want to both understand and apply the Jackson Structured Programming (JSP) approach to program design. It has been designed for trainee and experienced programmers, and students on BTEC courses (such as the Higher National Diploma in Computer Studies) and degree courses that incorporate the study of program design.

The aim is to present the principles and techniques of JSP in a way that will enable the reader to apply the method with confidence.

Structure of the book

The book first presents, in chapters 1–6, the basic method for relatively straightforward problems while stressing the important aspects through numerous examples and exercises. The production of logical data structures, being the basis of the method and the area where students may initially encounter difficulties, is dealt with at length. Chapter 4 then explains how the identification of corresponding components in the input and output structures enables them to be combined to form a program structure. The allocation of conditions and operations to this program structure is covered in chapter 5; conversion of the program structure with allocated conditions and operations into schematic logic (that is, a pseudocode representation) is then explained in chapter 6.

Since JSP does not presume upon any particular programming language, neither does this book. However, to illustrate the ease with which programs can be coded after they have been designed in a language-free manner, the appropriate coding rules for COBOL, PASCAL and BASIC are outlined in chapter 7.

After the basic techniques have been mastered, the reader may then proceed to the more difficult aspects. The concepts of processing more than one input file, including different types of merge problems, are examined in detail. The concepts of structure clashes and recognition problems, together with their solutions (that is, inversion and backtracking respectively) are examined in a practical manner. Interactive programs appear to be a special class of problem, so a separate chapter deals with the application of the method to such problems.

The book also illustrates the usefulness of the design method in respect of procedurisation, testing, documentation and amendment of existing programs.

Use of the book

To ensure that each technique is mastered as it is introduced, we strongly urge the reader to attempt all the exercises given at the end of most chapters, and to arrive at his/her own solution before turning to the solutions provided in appendix A.

Since this is primarily a book on program design, these solutions are normally given as program structure diagrams with allocated operations and conditions, or as schematic logic. However, having completed the design, the reader may wish to experience the satisfaction of running the program by translating certain solutions into a target language (see chapter 7).

Four case studies and their solutions are also provided in the appendixes. A note is included at the end of chapters 6, 9, 10 and 12, indicating that the appropriate case study may then be attempted. These extended problems can therefore be used for reinforcement and additional practice immediately after the appropriate chapter, or for revision purposes at a later stage.

Acknowledgements

It would be inappropriate to write a book on JSP without acknowledging the work of Michael Jackson, particularly his book *Principles of Program Design*. Our interest in Jackson's method was also stimulated by Brian Ratcliff of the University of Aston in Birmingham.

We would like to thank our colleagues in the Mathematics, Statistics and Computing Department, and staff from the Computer Services Department, of Liverpool Polytechnic for their advice, assistance and encouragement. Our thanks also to all those students who attended the lecture courses on which this book is based — their questions and comments have helped enormously.

1 The Importance of Program Design

1.1 Introduction

The importance of properly designed software of any kind, from the trivial application program to the most complex operating system, cannot be over-stressed. In these days when software production and maintenance costs are escalating in relation to total system costs and there is a shortage of skilled software producers, the computing profession can ill-afford to produce substandard software. Yet, much poor software is produced, mainly owing to poor problem definition and poor program design.

Much can be done to improve problem definition, and the problem of poor program design can be overcome by the adoption of formal methods of design.

To quote Wirth [*Communications of the ACM*, April 1971, p. 221] 'Programming courses should teach methods of design and construction, and the selected examples should be such that a gradual development can be nicely demonstrated.'

This text aims to satisfy these criteria by concentrating on a particular design method, namely Jackson Structured Programming (JSP). In this chapter, we discuss briefly the general requirements of a software design method and provide an overview of JSP.

1.2 Requirements of a software design method

A software design method is a set of basic principles and techniques that enables problems to be solved using a computer. Any design method worth using must have a set of rules to identify the class of problem that can be solved and to guide the problem solver in a step-by-step manner through the various stages of software production. It must emphasise that the solution of the problem is dependent on the transformation of the input data into results. The outcome of each stage in the design process should yield good documentation, allow progress to be assessed and give an early warning of errors. It is critically important that errors are diagnosed as early as possible before they become entrenched and consequently more difficult, and thus more costly, to remove.

1

The requirements of a software design method may be summarised as follows:

1. To enable correct programs to be produced.
2. To facilitate the organised control of software projects.
3. To facilitate the handling of large and/or complex projects.
4. To enable systematic methods to be applied rigorously by trained personnel.
5. To provide a method that is 'workable' within the intellectual limitations of the average programmer.
6. To afford techniques that can be taught and do not rely on inspiration or perspiration.

1.3 The characteristics of JSP

Jackson describes his own method as having the following characteristics:

1. It is non-inspirational; it depends little, or not at all, on invention and insight on the part of the designer.
2. It is rational; the design procedure is based on reasoned principles, and each step may be validated in the light of these principles.
3. It is teachable; people can be taught to practise the method and two or more programmers using the method to solve the same problem will arrive at substantially the same solution.
4. It is practical; the method itself is simple and easy to understand, and the designs produced can be implemented without difficulty in any ordinary programming environment.

1.4 The stages of JSP

The details of JSP are developed gradually throughout the book. In this section we merely describe the basic principles and design stages so that the reader may gain some insight into where each stage fits within the overall method.

The principles of JSP are as follows:

1. Analysis of the problem that the program is to solve, and the production of structure diagrams; data are usually the basis of the program, so data structures are created.
2. Analysis of the main programming tasks and the production of a program structure based on the data structures.
3. Definition of the tasks in terms of elementary operations and allocation of each of these to the component parts of the program structure.
4. Conversion (or translation) of the program structure and (allocated) operations into a computer programming language.

Specifically, to design a computer program we must:

1. Draw structure diagrams for each set of data such that the structures reflect the way in which the data are to be processed; we may call these 'logical data structures' to distinguish them from 'physical data structures' which take no account of the problem at hand.
2. Identify points of correspondence of a one-for-one nature between components of individual data structures.
3. Produce a program structure diagram using the same notation as for the data structures and based on the data structures, by combining them at the points of correspondence.
4. Where a single program structure cannot be produced directly from the data structures because of a 'structure clash', proceed to design two (or more) separate programs with communication via an intermediate file which corresponds to both program structures.
5. For each iteration and selection, construct appropriate conditions; where this is not possible use special techniques which overcome recognition problems.
6. Examine the specification and the conditions and from these draw up a list of basic program operations in plain language.
7. Allocate the conditions and operations to the appropriate components of the program structure.
8. Produce 'schematic logic' (pseudo-code) from the program structure.
9. Implement the schematic logic in a target high level programming language.

2 Data Structures

2.1 The JSP notation

For any programming problem (not involving parallel activities) structure diagrams may be drawn consisting of just three basic construct types:

- Sequence
- Iteration (loop)
- Selection (choice)

(a) The notation for a sequence is shown in figure 2.1.

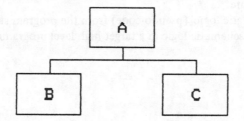

Figure 2.1

Component (box) A is a sequence. Boxes B and C represent component parts of the sequence. In this case they are not further defined and hence have no 'structure' of their own; they are known as elementary components.

In the above example, A is a sequence of the two components B followed by C. The notation could of course be extended for a sequence of any number of component parts.

(b) The notation for an iteration is shown in figure 2.2.

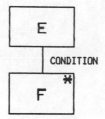

Figure 2.2

Component (box) E is an iteration. The box F is the iteration component part. E is an iteration of a number (possibly zero) of F's. The number of F's is controlled by the specified condition.

(c) The notation for a selection is shown in figure 2.3.

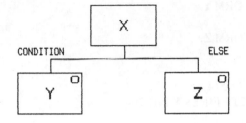

Figure 2.3

Box X is a selection. Boxes Y and Z are component parts of the selection.

In the above example, X is a selection (or choice) of Y or Z. Only the condition for the choice of Y is specified — if this condition is not true Z is chosen.

As for a sequence, the notation can be extended for any number of component parts (or choices). The final choice is always governed by the 'else' situation.

2.2 Data and procedures

Structure diagrams can be used to depict data and problem procedures. We will use simple COBOL statements to make this point.

Consider the sequence in section 2.1

procedure:
    A.
        B. MOVE 1 TO COUNT.
        C. ADD 2 TO TOTAL.

data:
      01 A.
         03 B PIC 9.
         03 C PIC X(4).

Consider the iteration in section 2.1

procedure:
    E.
        PERFORM F UNTIL CONDITION-1.
data:
      01 E.
         03 F PIC X(4) OCCURS N TIMES.

Finally consider the selection in section 2.1

procedure:
    X.

        IF CONDITION-FOR-Y

          PERFORM Y
        ELSE
          PERFORM Z.

data:
      01 X.
         03 Y PIC X(4).
         03 Z REDEFINES Y PIC 9(4).

2.3 Examples of how data structures are produced

The following examples show how a data structure may be produced from a narrative description using the three constructs, described above, in various combinations. As the examples are examined, notice that each component is of a unique type; that is, either a selection or an iteration or a sequence or an elementary component having no structure of its own. Notice also that a component cannot have a mixture of component parts; for example, an iteration may have only one iteration component part, and a selection may have only selection component parts.

(a) Consider a pack of playing cards as data. If the cards are not sorted the data structure may be represented as in figure 2.4.

    At this stage we do not include conditions on the structure diagram. However, there is no harm in considering what the condition should be. In this case, it is obviously UNTIL END OF PACK.

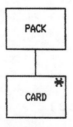

Figure 2.4

(b) If the pack was sorted by suit, all the spades, then the hearts, then the diamonds, then the clubs, we would need to show this division of suits and the sequence of their appearance in the pack. This is given in figure 2.5.

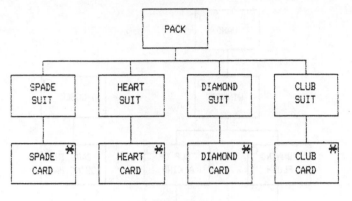

Figure 2.5

(c) Again, consider a pack of playing cards. Suppose we turn over the first card. If it is a picture card we win, otherwise we lose. The data structure for the pack is now as shown in figure 2.6.

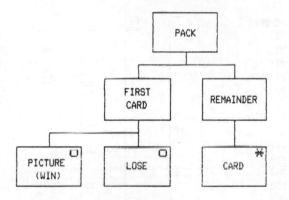

Figure 2.6

(d) In a game of 5 card poker, two hands are left in the game. Honest Joe has three aces and two kings. Dodgy George, therefore, has a hand that may be represented by figure 2.7.

(e) Let us now consider a computer file. A sales file contains a header record, followed by detail records grouped according to the month, with a total at the end of each month. At the end of the file there may or may not be a grand total record.

A sketch depicting a typical sales file may help you to visualise the structure. We list a typical file and then identify the order and grouping of the data by working from the top level. The overall structure can be developed by considering each level in turn, as illustrated with suitable abbreviations in figure 2.8.

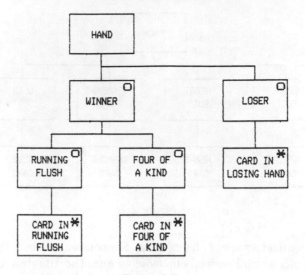

Figure 2.7

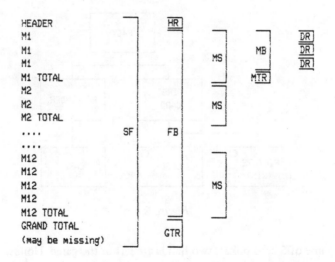

Figure 2.8

We perceive, at the top level, that the SALES FILE (SF) consists of three components — the HEADER RECORD (HR) followed by the FILE BODY (FB) and then the GRAND TOTAL RECORD (GTR). It is therefore a sequence.

Now consider the next level. HEADER RECORD needs no further refinement and from the narrative we know that GRAND TOTAL RECORD is a selection with elementary component parts; FILE BODY is an iteration of MONTHLY SECTION (MS).

Concentrating on MONTHLY SECTION reveals a sequence of MONTH BODY (MB) followed by MONTH TOTAL RECORD (MTR).

Finally MONTH BODY is an iteration of DETAIL RECORD (DR).

Thus, the data structure is as shown in figure 2.9.

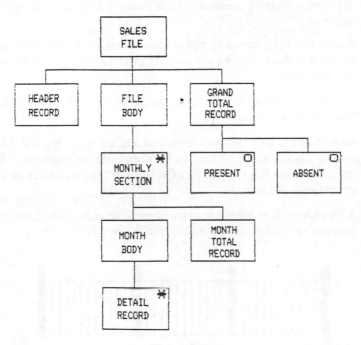

Figure 2.9

When considering later examples or attempting exercises, if you have difficulty visualising a data structure, then we strongly recommend the use of a sketch similar to that in figure 2.8. You may wish to devise your own notation, but note the repeated use of the same code (MS and DR) to identify the component part of an iteration.

2.4 Exercises

2.4.1. Suppose the pack of cards was sorted by value of card, such that we have all the aces first, followed by all the twos, then the threes and so on until the final group is all the kings. What would be an appropriate data structure?

2.4.2. From a shuffled pack, you deal a hand face upwards until you have dealt an ace. Draw a data structure diagram for the hand that you have dealt. What is the minimum number of cards in the hand?

2.4.3. The pack of cards is sorted by suit, but the order of the suits is not known. Draw a data structure diagram.

2.4.4. A book consists of a number of chapters followed by an appendix. Each chapter consists of a number of paragraphs and the appendix has a number of keyword sections consisting of one or more definitions. Draw the data structure.

2.4.5. A customer file is sorted by region code. There are a number of regions in the file and there could be any number of records per region. Draw the data structure.

2.4.6. The same customer file is sorted by credit limit code within region code. Draw the data structure.

2.4.7. An invoice has the customer's name and address at the top and the total amount payable at the bottom. In between there are a number of lines for individual items (we may call this the body of the invoice). Draw a data structure for the invoice.

2.4.8. A fence consists of a number of concrete posts each with 12 boards between each pair of posts, as shown in figure 2.10.

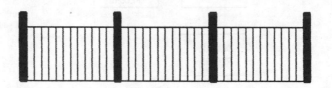

Figure 2.10

Draw a data structure diagram for the above fence.

2.4.9. Amend the above for a fence where the last section has only 6 boards.

2.4.10. The standard design for a house includes a specification as follows. The front of the house (looking at it from left to right) has a large window which may be Georgian style or a picture window, followed by a door which may or may not have a glazed upper section. If the door has no glazing it may be painted red or green; glazed doors are always green. After the door (on the right-hand side of the house) there are either two small windows or a large window. Draw a data structure for the front of the house.

2.4.11. In a 'fun run' a majority of the runners completed the course and of these a significant proportion recorded their best time. There was no discrimination between the sexes, but there were two categories of runner — 'beginner' and 'past-it'. Draw a data structure of all the competitors using the above information. Your solution does not have to reflect the order in which the competitors finished.

2.4.12. A magnetic tape contains production details as follows. For each machine group there are a number of detailed records followed by a total record; for each area there are a number of machine groups. At the end of the tape there may or may not be a grand total record. Draw a data structure for the magnetic tape file.

3 Data Structures for Particular Problems

3.1 Physical data structures and logical data structures

A physical data structure fully describes some data without taking into account any particular use to which the data may be put.

A logical data structure describes some data in respect of a particular use or for a certain problem. For example, the physical data structure of a pack of playing cards that is fully sorted (ace to king) for each suit, but with no particular suit order, is shown in figure 3.1.

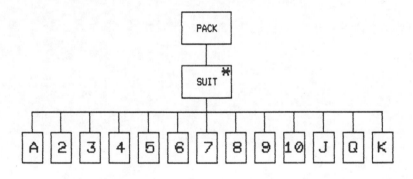

Figure 3.1

A logical data structure cannot deny any of the components of the physical structure and is essentially an extract of it. For example, given the same pack of cards, but with a problem specification of isolating the aces, we would draw the logical data structure shown in figure 3.2.

If the problem was to extract all the heart suit, then the logical data structure is as shown in figure 3.3.

It is stressed that, although the physical data structure remains unaltered, we may arrive at different logical structures depending on the problem. The logical structures must always be consistent with the physical data structure; that is, they must not violate the physical structure. You should convince yourself that this is true in the above example.

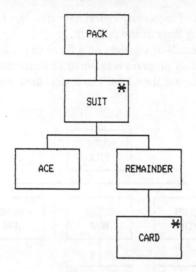

Figure 3.2

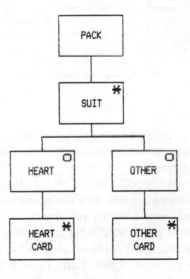

Figure 3.3

3.2 A logical data structure for a simple problem

Let us now consider certain aspects of logical data structures in the context of
producing a program. Eventually, we shall draw logical data structures for all
input and output files, combine these to produce a program structure and then
allocate conditions and operations (for example, print report headings) which can
easily be translated into a programming language. At this stage, we are concentra-

ting on the production of individual logical data structures, which reflect the structure and processing logic of the problem.

A file containing records of students on a three year course is sorted into ascending order of year. A program is required to count the number of second year students who have paid their fees. The logical data structure is shown in figure 3.4.

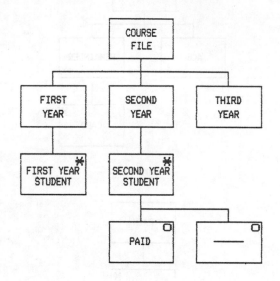

Figure 3.4

Note that this diagram reflects the way in which the data are to be processed, but does not contain any processing detail such as 'read student file' or 'increment student-paid count'.

Output from the program would contain, among other things, the required student total, but this element of data does not appear on the input file and therefore does not appear on the above structure.

The selection SECOND YEAR STUDENT is necessary because the way in which we are to process student depends on whether the appropriate data on the student record indicate payment of fees or not. We have introduced here the null elementary component (the selection part with a dash in) which may be used for the ELSE option.

The component FIRST YEAR is regarded as an iteration of student because we will have to process these records by reading past them. Although the physical data structure would indicate that THIRD YEAR is also an iteration of student, these records do not need to appear on the logical data structure. Omitting this component is allowed in the sense that we are not contradicting the physical structure. However, if a different problem required the processing of all the third year students before the first year students, then we would not be able to draw a logical data structure consistent with the physical organisation. Problems such as this are considered in later chapters.

3.3 Exercises

3.3.1. A file contains three different types of records (type 1, type 2, type 3). Records of type 1 are processed by summing the amounts. Records of type 2 are processed according to a region code – if the code is A the record is displayed, otherwise the first 20 characters only are displayed. Records of type 3 are ignored. Draw the logical data structure of the file in respect of the above problem.

3.3.2. A payroll file has records for individual employees containing a department code.

    (a) Draw a logical data structure in respect of a program to extract one specific department's data.

    (b) If the file is sorted into ascending order of department code, draw a revised logical data structure.

3.3.3. Consider a customer file sorted by credit limit code within region code. The region code may have a value of A, B or C only. What are the logical data structures in respect of the following?

    (a) A program to count the number of records.

    (b) A program to count the number of records in region A.

    (c) A program to count the number of records in region C.

    (d) A program to sum the amount due of all records with credit limit code = 1.

    (e) A program to print the names of customers who have a credit limit of 4 who are not in region A.

3.3.4. A criminal record file is purged (that is, redundant records are removed) according to the following criteria:

    (i) When the prisoner is released, for offences carrying a sentence of less than two years.

    (ii) 3 years after the prisoner is released, for offences carrying a sentence of two years or more; unless the offence is murder, when the record is not removed at all.

You may assume that murder will always carry a sentence of at least two years.

Draw a logical data structure in respect of the 'purging' program for each of the following:

    (a) The file is organised in ascending sequence of prison sentence term.

    (b) The file is organised into offence order (that is, all the burglaries together, all the murders together etc.).

    (c) The file is organised in alphabetic order of surname.

3.3.5. A report is to be produced. Each page contains 42 detail lines in addition to page headings and a total line. The total line includes appropriate text,

indicating that it may be a grand total or a cumulative carried forward
total. Draw the logical data structure for the report file.

3.3.6. Draw the logical data structure for a label print file where the labels are
'3 up' across the page. The labels may contain 3 or 4 lines of print.

You may assume that a row of labels can be constructed in memory
and that a complete row can be printed before moving on to the next one.

3.3.7. A program is required to print each record of a transaction file together
with an indication of the record type. In the file there may be three types
of batch — credits, debits and account descriptions. Each batch has a batch
header followed by any number of detail records. There may be any number of batches and they can occur in any order.

(a) Draw the logical data structure for the transaction file.
(b) Amend the above data structure to show that credit batches may
    contain 'cash' records and 'cheque' records in any order.
(c) Further amend the data structure to show that debit batches contain
    pairs of records — a sales record followed by a discount record.

3.3.8. A sales file contains a header record followed by details for several sales-
men. For each salesman there will be a header record followed by sales
detail records which are either cash or account.

(a) Draw the logical data structure for the sales file in respect of a program
    that is to process sales details of all salesmen.
(b) Amend the above data structure to show an optional totals record at
    the end of each group of salesman's records.
(c) Further amend the data structure to show that all sales values of £10
    or more attract a discount.

4 Program Structures

4.1 Identifying correspondences

A correct program structure will 'mirror' the data structures of its input and output. So we now consider how to produce a program structure by combining the logical data structures (at this stage we assume a maximum of one input and one output structure).

This means starting at the highest level and looking for components of the data structures that correspond in the sense that the whole of one component is used (or processed) to produce the whole of the other.

Particularly, the components should correspond in that the data represented by the corresponding components of the data structures must occur in the same order, and there should be the same number of each. Consider the structures shown in figure 4.1.

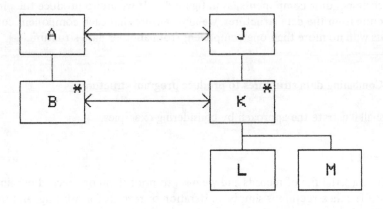

Figure 4.1

Starting from the top, A corresponds with J because there is one of each and we process A to obtain J. B corresponds with K if we process B to obtain K and the data which they represent can be shown diagrammatically as in figure 4.2.

17

Figure 4.2

Note that the data satisfy the rules:

1. Same order.
2. Same number of each.
3. Output derived from input.

Components B and K would not correspond in the cases shown in figure 4.3.

Figure 4.3

Having identified correspondences, we indicate them by drawing a line between the corresponding components, as in figure 4.1. If we are to produce the program structure from the data structures, we must ensure that each component corresponds with no more than one component from another data structure.

4.2 Combining data structures to produce program structures

We shall illustrate the approach by considering examples.

Example 1

We have a serial file of records and we wish to print them one record per line. The input file data structure is simply an iteration of records for printing, and the output file data structure an iteration of lines (each containing one record), as shown in figure 4.4.

Combining these data structures is easy because INPUT FILE corresponds with OUTPUT FILE and RECORD corresponds with LINE.

How so? In the first case, there is one input file that will be processed to produce one output file. In the second case, one record is processed to produce

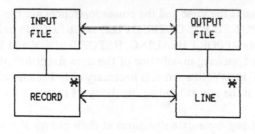

Figure 4.4

one line; and record and line are in the same order (record *n* of the input file will be printed on line *n*).

The components that correspond can now be combined to give the program structure common to both of the data structures exactly; see figure 4.5.

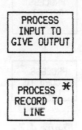

Figure 4.5

Example 2

Extending the above example, suppose we wanted to print a report heading at the start and a line containing a record count at the end. The data structures are shown in figure 4.6.

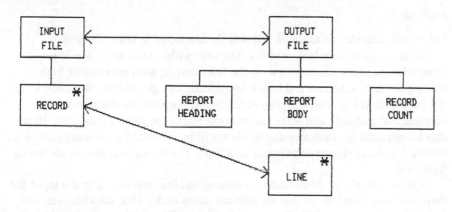

Figure 4.6

The input file remains the same and the correspondences are the same as in the first example (INPUT FILE to OUTPUT FILE and RECORD to LINE).

The components REPORT HEADING, REPORT BODY and RECORD COUNT, although appearing in only one of the data structures, do not cause any conflict. REPORT BODY, in a sense, is necessary only because of the need to distinguish between the report heading, the body of the report and the record count.

Then by combining these data structures at their points of correspondence we produce the program structure shown in figure 4.7.

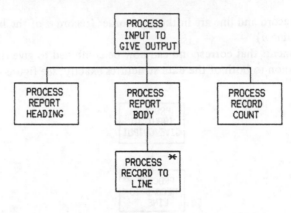

Figure 4.7

In this case the relative positions of the components without correspondences are easily determined from the output structure. Note that the program structure also retains the logic of the input structure, in that PROCESS INPUT TO GIVE OUTPUT can be regarded indirectly (through the component PROCESS REPORT BODY) as an iteration of PROCESS RECORD TO LINE.

Example 3

Let us now consider an example that will be developed in later chapters.

We have a sales file which is sorted into year within sales area code. It is required to produce a report to show the sales details, with appropriate highlighting for low, moderate and high sales (that is, a single exclamation mark when the sales value is less than 100, two exclamation marks when the sales value is between 100 and 300, and three exclamation marks for greater than 300). Headings are required for each area and totals are to be produced at relevant control breaks, that is, at change of year and area code. The data structures are shown in figure 4.8.

In respect of the problem under consideration, for each record in the input file there are three possibilities that are relevant: sales under 100, sales between 100 and 300, and sales over 300. There are also three different lines of print, depend-

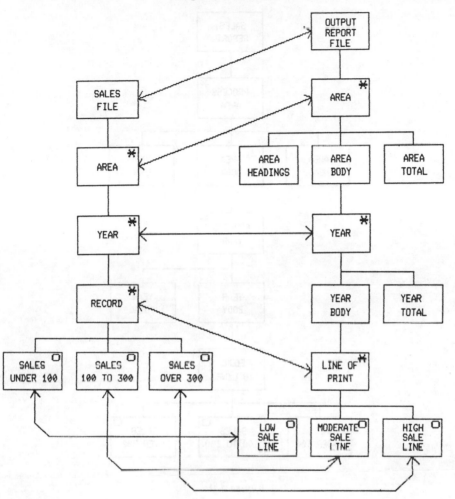

Figure 4.8

ing on whether the sales are low, moderate or high. Thus both data structures contain a selection at the lowest level.

Once again, using the criteria of 'processing the whole of one component to produce the other, and order and number of data', identifying the correspondences is straightforward. Fortunately, both files are sorted by year within area code and each detail line of print is obtained by processing the corresponding sales record. The positions of the non-corresponding components in the program structure are given by the output structure — see figure 4.9.

Since it can be taken as read, we shall not include 'PROCESS' in naming program structure components from now on.

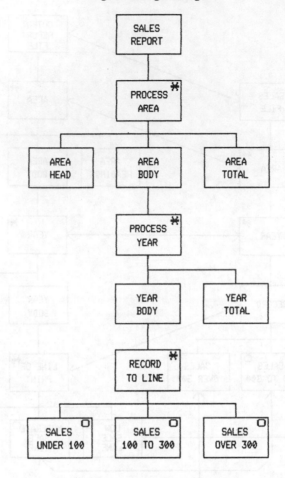

Figure 4.9

The program structure again retains the logic of both data structures. You should be able to perceive the SALES FILE structure through intermediate components.

Example 4

A personnel file contains records of factory and office workers. A report, with headings, giving details of the factory workers is required. The data structures are given in figure 4.10.

A comparison with the previous example raises two questions.

Why have we not included the selection parts on the REPORT FILE? Simply because there are no office workers' details on the output file.

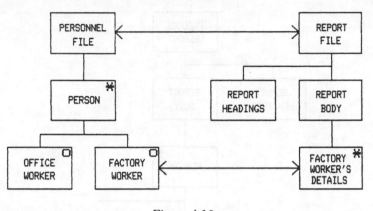

Figure 4.10

Why does FACTORY WORKER'S DETAILS correspond with FACTORY WORKER? Simply because the correspondence satisfies our criteria; FACTORY WORKER'S DETAILS does not correspond with PERSON since, in general, there will be fewer FACTORY WORKER'S DETAILS lines than PERSON records.

It is also a little more difficult to produce the program structure. The position of PERSON relative to REPORT HEADINGS and REPORT BODY is not obvious from the data structures, and the component part indicators of corresponding components do not match.

We overcome these problems by always merging the data structures such that:

1. Corresponding components are combined.
2. The logic of the data structures, as defined by the problem specification, is retained.

PERSON cannot be a sequence of REPORT HEADINGS and REPORT BODY, as this would include headings for each person and contradict the structure of REPORT FILE. However, making REPORT BODY an iteration of PERSON retains the required logic. The specification also requires us to retain the two selection parts, hence FACTORY WORKER'S DETAILS is combined with FACTORY WORKER as a selection part of PERSON. The program structure is shown in figure 4.11.

Again, you should be able to perceive the data structures in the program structure. As far as the output file is concerned, REPORT BODY remains an iteration of FACTORY WORKER because FACTORY WORKER is part of the iteration part PERSON.

It should be stressed that the program structure must always be derived from the data structures. As mentioned in chapter 1, one of the requirements of a software design method is that errors should be identified as soon as possible. Logical data structures that are difficult to combine may well, though not necessarily, contain errors. If you have any difficulty combining data structures or cannot find correspondences, first check that the logical data structures are correct in

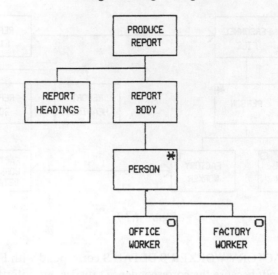

Figure 4.11

respect of the problem to be solved. The temptation to omit or introduce components arbitrarily should be resisted in favour of re-examining the data structures.

Unfortunately there are times when the data structures are correct but it is still not possible to produce a correct program structure. This occurs when data structures contradict or clash with each other. Even this situation can be resolved, as we shall see in chapter 9.

Now for some more exercises. Data structures are to be produced followed by program structures based entirely on the data structures.

4.3 Exercises

4.3.1. A production file contains a number of records about machines, indicating whether or not they are due for replacement. It is required to produce a duplicate file with one extra record at the end, containing a count of the machines that are due for replacement.

   (a) Draw the logical data structures and show the correspondences.
   (b) Combine the data structures to produce a program structure.

4.3.2. A hospital file contains records of staff and patients sorted into ascending order of surname within ward. It is required to print all the names of the staff in ward order, with a heading at the start of each ward.

   Draw the two logical data structures and show the correspondences between them. Hence, produce a program structure.

4.3.3. A personnel file is sorted by grade of staff and contains records of employees' qualifications. It is required to produce a list of the number of staff in each grade who possess a degree. The record layout for the personnel file is as follows:

character positions 1-3   Grade of staff
                4-20   Name
                21   No. of 'O' levels
                22   No. of 'A' levels
                23   Degree (Y or N)

The output required is of the form:

XYZ COMPANY – EMPLOYEES WITH DEGREES

GRADE	NUMBER
1	23
6	15
12	16
15	0
100	10
TOTAL	64

(a) Draw the logical data structure for the personnel file.
(b) Draw the logical data structure for the report file.
(c) Combine the data structures to produce a program structure.

Hints
Not all of the detail contained in the input record is pertinent to the problem at hand. Remember that you are drawing logical data structures that describe the data in respect of this particular problem.

A small sketch of sample data for both logical data structures may help (see chapter 2), particularly when identifying correspondences. It should be apparent that certain groups of records in the input file correspond to certain lines on the output.

4.3.4. A product file contains a number of product records. Each record contains an area code, a district code, a product code and a value. The file is sorted into product within district within area. A program is required to select certain product codes, and produce a report showing district and area totals of the values of the selected products in the order implied by the product file.

    Draw the two logical data structures and show the correspondences between them. Hence produce a program structure.

4.3.5. A student application file contains records which hold the status of applicants. The file is sorted into ascending order of course code. For each course there may be records of applicants who have merely been offered a place, followed by records of applicants who have been offered a place and accepted it, followed by records of applicants who have been rejected.

(a) It is required to print a listing, containing a report for each course of all rejected applicants, in ascending order of course code. The reports contain a heading followed by the various applicants' names (one per line) followed by a total of such names. Draw the logical data structures and then combine them to produce a program structure. Note that the logic of the problem means that we need not differentiate between the batches of applicants who have been offered places and the batches of applicants who have accepted places.

(b) It is further required to produce a file containing records of accepted applicants in ascending order of course code. Draw logical data structures for the input file and both output files, indicate correspondences and hence produce a revised program structure. This is the first problem that you have encountered with more than one output. You should draw correspondences between each output file and the input file, before combining all three to produce the program structure.

4.3.6. A payroll file is sorted by employee number and contains records of employees' pay details. Included in each employee record are a group of ten deductions which are specified by a code followed by an amount. It is required to produce a report showing those employees who pay deduction code 20 with amounts greater than £1. The format of the output is:

XYZ AUTHORITY − EMPLOYEES PAYING UNION FEES

NAME	AMOUNT
B JONES	1.10
F SMITH	3.50
R BROWN	2.75
TOTAL	XXX.XX

(a) Draw the logical data structure for the payroll file. There is at most one occurrence of deduction code 20 with an amount greater than £1 in a record. If present it can be in any of the ten elements of the deduction group.

Ideally we should stop examining the deduction group once the required deduction has been found. However, to avoid using an advanced technique, explained in chapter 10, you may assume an examination of all elements of the group.

(b) Draw the logical data structure for the report file.
(c) Combine the data structures to produce a program structure.

5 Elementary Program Operations and Conditions

5.1 Listing the conditions

When we are happy with our program structure, we are then in a position to think about the elementary program operations that must be included within the structure, and the conditions that control the iterations and selections. First we identify and list the conditions.

For each iteration we require a terminating condition, so we ask:

'How will the end of the iteration be detected?'
or
'What condition must always be true for the iteration to continue?'.

Note that the answer to the first question gives the terminating condition directly, but the answer to the second gives the condition for the iteration to continue, which must therefore be negated.

Using the 'sales report' program structure from chapter 4 (see figure 5.1), let us list the conditions for the iterations.

The iteration SALES REPORT is concluded when there are no more AREAs to process. Or put another way, the iteration continues while there are AREAs to process. In other words the condition is

process SALES REPORT until end of sales file.

Note that, at this stage, the conditions are written in a form that is independent of any programming language (that is, end of sales file).

The definition of an iteration (see chapter 2) allows for SALES REPORT to be an iteration of zero PROCESS AREAs (that is, the loop may not be entered). To allow for this we must assume that the condition is tested at the start of the loop. While there is a case to be made for an iteration construct of at least one occurrence, as well as the one we have already defined, we shall not draw this distinction.

The iteration AREA BODY continues while there are YEARs of the current AREA to process. How can we detect that there are no more YEARs of the current AREA? Clearly there are no more YEARs of any AREA at the end of the file, so that must come into it. Further, when a new AREA is to be processed, there are no more YEARs for the old AREA. The condition then is a compound one:

process AREA BODY until end of sales file or a change of area.

27

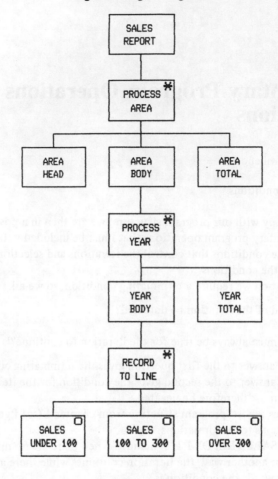

Figure 5.1

In this nested loop situation, the condition for the outer loop should always be included as part of the condition for the inner loop. This ensures that the inner loop will eventually terminate even though 'a change of area' may not be detected.

One can use similar reasoning to determine the condition for the iteration YEAR BODY. One recognises the end of the records that relate to a particular YEAR for a particular AREA when the YEAR changes or when the AREA changes or when the end of the file is reached. So:

> process YEAR BODY until end of sales file or a change of area or a change of year.

For the selections, we ask:

> 'What must be true for each of the options?'
> 'Are the conditions mutually exclusive?'
> 'Is the last option covered by ELSE?'

For the selection RECORD TO LINE, we need two conditions. There are three choices, but we have made the decision that the last selection part shall always be conditionless (that is, will be reached by ELSE). The conditions are:

> select SALES UNDER 100 if sales value < 100
> else select SALES 100 TO 300 if sales value $< = 300$
> else select SALES OVER 300.

This gives a condition list as follows:

> C1 — Until end of sales file
> C2 — Until end of sales file or change of area
> C3 — Until end of sales file or change of area or change of year
> C4 — If sales value < 100
> C5 — If sales value $< = 300$ (and $> = 100$)

5.2 Listing the elementary program operations

The elementary program operations can be listed by studying the program specification and taking cognisance of the program structure and conditions. What do we mean by elementary program operations? Here we will not consider the operations in terms of any particular programming language, but rather, entities that we know will be very easily converted to one or more program language statements.

We can tackle this part of the design in steps.

1. List the program initialisation and finalisation operations such as open and close files.
2. Identify the input records or components and hence list the input operations.
3. Identify the output records or components and hence list the output operations.
4. Identify any computations or transformations from input to output necessary to produce the detailed aspects of the required results.
5. List any detailed initialisation operations that will be required.
6. List any operations necessary to support the condition list.

In our 'sales report' program, the program initialisation and finalisation operations are:

1. Open files.
2. Close files.
3. Stop.

There is only one input operation:

4. Read a sales file record.

The principal operations to produce the required output are:

5. Print area headings.
6. Print area total.

7. Print year total.
8. Print a sales under 100 line.
9. Print a sales 100 to 300 line.
10. Print a sales over 300 line.

Operations 6 and 7 require some computation, hence:

11. Add to area total.
12. Add to year total.

The above, in turn, require initialisation operations:

13. Initialise area total to zero.
14. Initialise year total to zero.

Finally two operations are necessary because we need to be able to compare the AREA (or YEAR) of the record just read with the AREA (or YEAR) currently being processed. This is in order to construct the conditions 'change of year' and 'change of area' for the iterations YEAR BODY and AREA BODY.

15. Store area code.
16. Store year.

5.3 Allocating the conditions and operations

Allocation of the conditions is simple. We simply draw up a condition list and then write the appropriate reference above and to the right of the iteration or selection component part, as illustrated by the 'sales report' program structure (figure 5.2).

Allocation of the program operations takes more thought, but should not present any difficulties. If we find difficulty deciding where a particular operation is to be performed in respect of a program structure, there are three possible causes:

1. We do not need the operation, in which case we should re-examine the problem specification.
2. The program structure is deficient, in which case we must go back to the data structures.
3. The operation implies a condition, in which case we need to be more specific in our choice of operations.

Figure 5.2 shows the 'sales report' program structure with the operation numbers added to it in appropriate places. We shall now discuss how the decisions for allocation were arrived at. Basically, for each operation we ask two questions:

1. How many times and where in the program structure should the operation be executed? This identifies the component.
2. Should it be executed at the beginning, the middle or the end of the identified component?

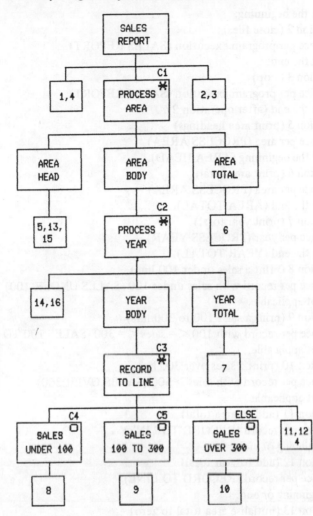

Figure 5.2

All operations are allocated to elementary components. In some cases the component already exists (for example, 6 is allocated to AREA TOTAL); in othe cases we effectively create a component (for example, the allocation of 2 and 3). When allocating an operation to a component already containing operations, you should ascertain its correct position relative to those already allocated (see operation 3 below).

Let us ask the above questions of the operations. We will leave operation number 4 for the moment.

Operation 1 (open files)
    Once per program execution (SALES REPORT)

At the beginning.

Operation 2 (close files)

Once per program execution (SALES REPORT)

At the end.

Operation 3 (stop)

Once per program execution (SALES REPORT)

At the end (after operation 2).

Operation 5 (print area headings)

Once per area (PROCESS AREA)

At the beginning (AREA HEAD).

Operation 6 (print area total)

Once per area (PROCESS AREA)

At the end (AREA TOTAL).

Operation 7 (print year total)

Once per year (PROCESS YEAR)

At the end (YEAR TOTAL).

Operation 8 (print a sales under 100 line)

Once per record with sales under 100 (SALES UNDER 100)

Not applicable.

Operation 9 (print a sales 100 to 300 line)

Once per record with $100 <= sales <= 300$ (SALES 100 TO 300)

Not applicable.

Operation 10 (print a sales over 300 line)

Once per record with sales > 300 (SALES OVER 300)

Not applicable.

Operation 11 (add to area total)

Once per record (RECORD TO LINE)

Beginning or end.

Operation 12 (add to year total)

Once per record (RECORD TO LINE)

Beginning or end.

Operation 13 (initialise area total to zero)

Once per area (PROCESS AREA)

At the beginning (AREA HEAD).

Operation 14 (initialise year total to zero)

Once per year (PROCESS YEAR)

At the beginning.

Operation 15 (store area code)

Once per area (PROCESS AREA)

At the beginning (AREA HEAD).

Operation 16 (store year)

Once per year (PROCESS YEAR)

At the beginning.

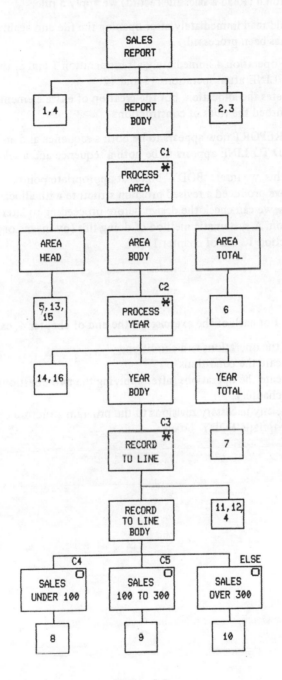

Figure 5.3

For operation 4 (Read a sales file record) we apply a rule:

> We should read immediately after opening the file and again as soon as a record has been processed.

So we allocate operation 4 immediately after operation 1 and at the end of RECORD TO LINE after operations 11 and 12.

This completes the allocation, but the creation of extra elementary component boxes has disturbed the rules of construction:

> SALES REPORT now appears to be both a sequence and an iteration
> RECORD TO LINE appears to be both a sequence and a selection.

To overcome this, we insert 'BODY' boxes at appropriate points; see figure 5.3.

Once we have produced a revised program structure with allocated operations and conditions, we can check the design before proceeding to later stages of program production. A systematic method of doing this (by means of a trace table) is shown in section 13.1.2 of chapter 13.

5.4 Exercises

5.4.1 to 5.4.6. For each of the exercises at the end of chapter 4, except 4.3.5(a):

(a) List the operations and conditions.
(b) Allocate the conditions.
(c) Allocate the operations (after applying the two questions discussed in this chapter).
(d) Make any necessary revisions to the program structure by inserting appropriate 'BODY' boxes.

6 Schematic Logic

6.1 Production of schematic logic (pseudo-code)

Schematic logic is a pseudo-code representation of the program structure with allocated operations and conditions. We will first produce schematic logic, then code the program in a high level programming language. Most programmers find it easier to translate the pseudo-code, rather than the program structure diagram, into the target language. Furthermore, when using one of the more advanced JSP techniques (covered in chapter 10), we shall find it necessary to amend the schematic logic, by introducing additional operations and conditions, without changing the program structure.

Let us describe the production of schematic logic for each of the three basic constructs, then put it all together for a whole program.

(a) Sequence – see figure 6.1

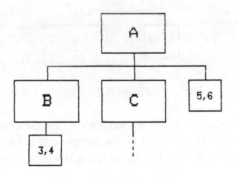

Figure 6.1

Here, A is a sequence of B (which has two operations, 3 then 4) followed by C (of unknown construct type) followed by operation 5 then operation 6.

The schematic logic is:

```
A SEQ              [construct-name type]
   B
```

```
          DO 3,4
       B  END
       C  . . . .          [component C is not defined
          : : : :            but it has a start and an
       C  END                end and comes after B]
          DO 5, 6
       A  END
```

Elementary components are shown as construct-name without type (for example, B). Elementary operations are shown as DO statements either with or without operation descriptions. For example

```
       DO 1, 4
```

or

```
       DO 1   [open files
       DO 4   [read a sales file record
```

(b) Iteration – see figure 6.2

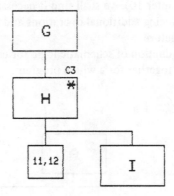

Figure 6.2

Here, G is an iteration of H, which is a sequence of the elementary component with operations 11 and 12, followed by the component I. Remember that it is component G that is the iteration construct, not H which is the component part of the iteration.

The schematic logic is:

```
       G  ITER UNTIL C3        [construct-name type condition]
          H  SEQ
             DO 11, 12
             I  . . . .
                : : : :
```

```
      I END
    H END
  G END
```

(c) Selection – see figure 6.3

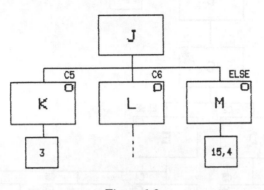

Figure 6.3

Here, J is a selection of K (which has the operation 3), or L (of unknown construct type), or M (which has operation 15 then operation 4). Recall that with a selection, the last component part has no specified condition; it is controlled by the 'else' situation (that is, when the other conditions are all false).

The schematic logic is:

```
J  SEL  IF  C5          [construct-name type condition]
  K
    DO 3
  K END
J  ELSE 1 IF C6          [name 1st alternative condition]
  L . . . .
    : : : :
  L END
J  ELSE 2               [name 2nd (last) alternative
  M                          no condition]
    DO 15, 4
  M END
J  END
```

In the three examples above you will notice how the indentation matches the program structure. The convention used here, and in the following examples, is to indent by two spaces in the schematic logic for each level of the structure. You may decide to emphasise the levels of structure by using deeper indentation.

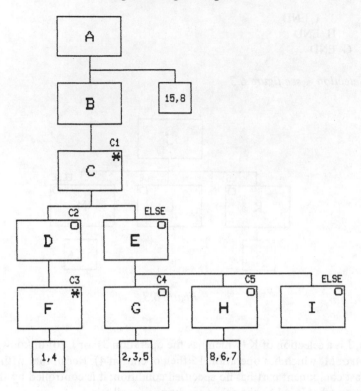

Figure 6.4

(d) An example of all three combined – see figure 6.4

Sometimes, as illustrated by I above, a component part of a selection has no elementary operations. In this case we still include the construct in our schematic logic (possibly with a comment to emphasise the 'passive' component).

The schematic logic is shown in figure 6.5.

6.2 Schematic logic for a complete program

Can we now tackle the production of schematic logic for the program structure for the 'sales report' program? You will find the program structure with allocated operations and conditions in figure 5.3. The schematic logic is shown in figure 6.6.

Check with the program structure (figure 5.3) in chapter 5. Notice how the indentation of the schematic logic matches the number of levels in the program structure.

```
A SEQ
  B ITER UNTIL C1
    C SEL IF C2
      D ITER UNTIL C3
        F
          DO 1,4
        F END
      D END
    C ELSE 1
      E SEL IF C4
        G
          DO 2,3,5
        G END
      E ELSE 1 IF C5
        H
          DO 8,6,7
        H END
      E ELSE 2
        I
          [note - no operations
        I END
      E END
    C END
  B END
  DO 15,8
A END
```

Figure 6.5

6.3 Exercises

6.3.1 to 6.3.6. The exercises at the end of chapter 5 asked you to produce program structures with allocated operations and conditions. For each of these,
produce the schematic logic. You will note that the solutions include descriptions for each condition and elementary operation, as in figure 6.6; you
may omit these descriptions.

If you wish, you may now attempt the case study in appendix B.

```
SALES REPORT SEQ
  DO 1    [open files
  DO 4    [read a sales file record
  REPORT BODY ITER UNTIL C1   [end of sales file
    PROCESS AREA SEQ
      AREA HEAD
        DO 5     [print area headings
        DO 13    [initialise area total to zero
        DO 15    [store area code
      AREA HEAD END
      AREA BODY ITER UNTIL C2   [end of sales file
                                 or change of area
        PROCESS YEAR SEQ
          DO 14   [initialise year total to zero
          DO 16   [store year
          YEAR BODY ITER UNTIL C3   [end of sales file
                  or change of area or change of year
            RECORD TO LINE SEQ
              RECORD TO LINE BODY SEL IF C4   [if sales
                                        value < 100
                SALES UNDER 100
                  DO 8    [print a sales under 100 line
                SALES UNDER 100 END
              RECORD TO LINE BODY ELSE 1 IF C5   [if sales
                        value <= 300 (and >= 100)
                SALES 100 TO 300
                  DO 9    [print a sales 100 to 300 line
                SALES 100 TO 300 END
              RECORD TO LINE BODY ELSE 2
                SALES OVER 300
                  DO 10   [print a sales over 300 line
                SALES OVER 300 END
              RECORD TO LINE BODY END
              DO 11 [add to area total
              DO 12 [add to year total
              DO 4    [read a sales file record
            RECORD TO LINE END
          YEAR BODY END
          YEAR TOTAL
            DO 7    [print year total
          YEAR TOTAL END
        PROCESS YEAR END
      AREA BODY END
      AREA TOTAL
        DO 6    [print area total
      AREA TOTAL END
    PROCESS AREA END
  REPORT BODY END
  DO 2    [close files
  DO 3    [stop
SALES REPORT END
```

Figure 6.6

7 Implementation in a High Level Programming Language

7.1 From schematic logic to a target language

The production of schematic logic, an elementary program operation list and condition list, essentially concludes the design stage. It remains only to translate these into a high level programming language. This involves:

1. Coding the declaration part of the program (as required by COBOL and PASCAL for example).
2. Implementing the schematic constructs — SEQ, SEL and ITER — using control constructs provided by the target language.
3. Translating each elementary operation and condition into the target language, bearing in mind that certain operations will require more than one program statement.

We shall illustrate this coding process for PASCAL, COBOL and BASIC. You may restrict your attention to the language(s) with which you are familiar. For each language we provide rules for implementation of the three basic constructs using the schematic examples from the previous chapter with 'OPERATION N' and 'CONDITION CN' denoting the appropriate coding for 'DO N' and 'CN'; then we illustrate the complete process by producing a working program for the 'sales report' problem.

Though the reader may adopt different conventions regarding indentation, the use of lower and upper case and the amount of schematic logic retained in the program as comments, it is suggested that the control logic of the rules given in the following sections should be adhered to. The experienced programmer will observe that there are obvious alternatives to the coding rules; we have used rules in this chapter which retain the structure of the schematic logic.

As can be seen from the following sections, converting the schematic constructs into a target language is a 'mechanical' process based on simple rules. Software packages that perform this process are now widely available. Typically, a JSP preprocessor requires input in the form of a declaration section, elementary operation list and condition list, all in the target language, followed by the schematic logic. The resulting output is a complete, coded program.

7.2 PASCAL as target language

The block structure of PASCAL is identical to that used in the schematic logic; their control constructs are almost identical — the only difference being the operation of the controlling predicates in the ITER and WHILE constructs (see below). The PASCAL code will therefore closely resemble the schematic logic.

(a) Sequence and elementary component

The sequence parts are retained in the same order as they appear in the schematic logic — see figure 7.1.

```
A SEQ                    (* a seq *)
  B                        (* b *)
    DO 3,4                   OPERATION 3
  B END                      OPERATION 4
  C ....                   (* b end *)
  ::::                     (* c .... *)
  C END                    ::::::
  DO 5,6                   (* c end *)
A END                      OPERATION 5
                           OPERATION 6
                         (* a end *)
```

Figure 7.1

Hence the rules for coding a sequence or elementary component are as follows.

1. At the start:

   create a comment, such as (* component name seq *) or
   (* component name *).

2. At the end:

   create a comment, such as (* component name end *).

(b) Iteration

PASCAL provides both a 'WHILE condition DO statement(s)' construct and a 'REPEAT statement(s) UNTIL condition' construct. The condition in the REPEAT construct is tested at the end of the loop. The iteration will therefore always occur at least once. Since it does not allow for zero occurrences, the REPEAT statement should not be used to code the ITER construct.

The WHILE statement, with the condition tested at the head of the loop, does allow for zero or more occurrences. However, for the ITER construct the iteration stops when the condition is true; for the WHILE statement the iteration stops when the condition is false. The ITER construct is therefore coded by means of the WHILE statement with the negation of the ITER condition — see figure 7.2.

```
G ITER UNTIL C3              (* g iter *)
  H SEQ                      WHILE NOT (CONDITION C3) DO
    DO 11,12                 BEGIN
    I ....                     (* h seq *)
    ::::                         OPERATION 11
    I END                        OPERATION 12
  H END                        (* i .... *)
G END                            ::::::
                                 (* i end *)
                               (* h end *)
                             END ;
                             (* g end *)
```

Figure 7.2

The coding rules for an iteration are as follows.

1. At the start:

   create a comment, such as (* component name iter *);
   use the WHILE construct with the negation of the ITER condition.

2. At the end:

   create a comment, such as (* component name end *).

(c) Selection

The SEL...ELSE... construct translates directly into the PASCAL 'IF condition
THEN statement(s) ELSE statement(s)' construct — see figure 7.3.

```
J SEL IF C5                  (* j sel *)
  K                          IF CONDITION C5 THEN
    DO 3                       (* k *)
  K END                          OPERATION 3
J ELSE 1 IF C6                 (* k end *)
  L ....                     (* j else 1 *)
  ::::                       ELSE IF CONDITION C6 THEN
  L END                      BEGIN
J ELSE 2                       (* l .... *)
  M                              ::::
    DO 15,4                    (* l end *)
  M END                      END
J END                        (* j else 2 *)
                             ELSE
                             BEGIN
                               (* m *)
                                 OPERATION 15
                                 OPERATION 4
                               (* m end *)
                             END ;
                             (* j end *)
```

Figure 7.3

The coding rules for a selection are as follows.

1. At the start:

> create a comment, such as (* component name sel *);
> use the IF . . . THEN part of the IF . . . THEN . . . ELSE . . . construct
> with the appropriate condition from the condition list.

2. At ELSE n:

> create a comment, such as (* component name else n *);
> use the ELSE IF . . . THEN part of the IF . . . THEN . . . ELSE . . .
> construct with the appropriate condition from the condition list, except
> for the last ELSE n where there is no condition.

3. At the end:

> create a comment, such as (* component name end *).

(d) Complete program

We shall now code a complete program (see figure 6.6 for schematic logic of the
'sales report' example) using the following approach.

1. Inspect the problem specification and hence declare those variables required
   for input and output, such as SALESREC, SALESFILE and REPORTFILE.
2. Inspect the elementary operations and conditions and hence declare any
   additional data items that will be required, such as STOREDYEAR.
3. Code the executable part of the program from the schematic logic, using the
   above rules for the control constructs and translating operations and conditions
   into PASCAL. For example

> 5. Print area headings
>   becomes
> WRITELN (REPORTFILE, 'AREA ',AREA) ;
> WRITELN (REPORTFILE) ;

As each operation and condition is coded:

(i)   Check that appropriate variables have been declared.
(ii) To prevent recoding of an operation or condition already used and to ensure
     that they are all eventually coded, tick each one off on the appropriate list.

As can be seen from the above example and the program shown in figure 7.4,
an elementary operation may require more than one program statement.

Note that the following solution assumes that the last record on the input file
is a dummy record (sentinel) with Z as the area code. End of file can then be
detected by AREA = 'Z'.

```
00100      PROGRAM SALES (SALESFILE,REPORTFILE) ;
00200
00300      TYPE
00400        RECORDTYPE =
00500          RECORD
00600            AREA            : CHAR ;
00700            YEAR            : 0..99 ;
00800            SALESPRODUCT    : PACKED ARRAY [1..20] OF CHAR ;
00900            SALESAMOUNT     : 0..999 ;
01000          END ;
01100
01200      VAR
01300        STOREDAREA          : CHAR ;
01400        STOREDYEAR          : 0..99 ;
01500        AREATOTAL,YEARTOTAL : 0..99999 ;
01600        SALESREC            : RECORDTYPE ;
01700        SALESFILE           : FILE OF RECORDTYPE ;
01800        REPORTFILE          : TEXT ;
01900
02000      (* sales report seq *)
02100      BEGIN
02200        RESET (SALESFILE) ;
02300        REWRITE (REPORTFILE) ;
02400        READ (SALESFILE,SALESREC) ;
02500        WITH SALESREC DO
02600        (* report body iter *)
02700        WHILE NOT (AREA = 'Z') DO
02800        BEGIN
02900          (* process area seq *)
03000            (* area head *)
03100              WRITELN (REPORTFILE,'AREA   ',AREA) ;
03200              WRITELN (REPORTFILE) ;
03300              AREATOTAL := 0 ;
03400              STOREDAREA := AREA ;
03500            (* area head end *)
03600            (* area body iter *)
03700            WHILE NOT ((AREA = 'Z')
03800                        OR (STOREDAREA <> AREA)) DO
03900            BEGIN
04000              (* process year seq *)
04100                YEARTOTAL := 0 ;
04200                STOREDYEAR := YEAR ;
04300              (* year body iter *)
04400              WHILE NOT ((AREA = 'Z')
04500                          OR (STOREDAREA <> AREA)
04600                          OR (STOREDYEAR <> YEAR)) DO
04700              BEGIN
04800                (* record to line seq *)
04900                  (* record to line body sel *)
05000                  IF SALESAMOUNT < 100 THEN
05100                    (* sales under 100 *)
05200                      WRITELN (REPORTFILE,SALESPRODUCT:20,
05300                              SALESAMOUNT:8,' !')
05400                    (* sales under 100 end *)
05500                  (* record to line body else 1 *)
05600                  ELSE IF SALESAMOUNT <= 300 THEN
05700                    (* sales 100 to 300 *)
05800                      WRITELN (REPORTFILE,SALESPRODUCT:20,
05900                              SALESAMOUNT:8,' !!')
06000                    (* sales 100 to 300 end *)
06100                  (* record to line body else 2 *)
```

Figure 7.4 (above and overleaf)

```
06200                          ELSE
06300                             (* sales over 300 *)
06400                             WRITELN (REPORTFILE,SALESPRODUCT:20,
06500                                     SALESAMOUNT:8,'  !!!') ;
06600                             (* sales over 300 end *)
06700                          (* record to line body end *)
06800                          AREATOTAL := AREATOTAL + SALESAMOUNT ;
06900                          YEARTOTAL := YEARTOTAL + SALESAMOUNT ;
07000                          READ (SALESFILE,SALESREC) ;
07100                       (* record to line end *)
07200                    END ;
07300                    (* year body end *)
07400                    (* year total *)
07500                       WRITELN (REPORTFILE) ;
07600                       WRITELN (REPORTFILE,'YEAR TOTAL ':23,
07700                               YEARTOTAL:5) ;
07800                       WRITELN (REPORTFILE) ;
07900                    (* year total end *)
08000                 (* process year end *)
08100              END ;
08200              (* area body end *)
08300              (* area total *)
08400                 WRITELN (REPORTFILE) ;
08500                 WRITELN (REPORTFILE,'AREA TOTAL ':23,
08600                         AREATOTAL:5) ;
08700                 WRITELN (REPORTFILE) ;
08800                 WRITELN (REPORTFILE) ;
08900              (* area total end *)
09000           (* process area end *)
09100        END ;
09200        (* report body end *)
09300     END.
09400     (* sales report end *)
```

7.3 COBOL as target language

The following examples illustrate how the schematic logic can be translated directly into COBOL code. We have not used the PERFORM verb in the coding rules because to do so would give a disjointed translation. A performed routine would not appear in the same relative position within the COBOL code as that of the corresponding pseudo-code within the schematic logic. Chapter 11 gives reasons why the use of PERFORM is not recommended when using the more advanced features of JSP, which are described in chapters 9 and 10.

(a) Sequence and elementary component

The sequence parts are retained in the same order as they appear in the schematic logic — see figure 7.5.

The coding rules for a sequence or elementary component are as follows.

1. At the start:

   use the paragraph name COMPONENT-NAME-SEQ or COMPONENT-NAME.

```
A SEQ                    A-SEQ.
  B                        B.
     DO 3,4                    OPERATION 3
  B END                        OPERATION 4
  C ....                   B-END.
    ::::                   C-.....
  C END                        ::::
     DO 5,6               C-END.
A END                         OPERATION 5
                              OPERATION 6
                         A-END.
```

Figure 7.5

2. At the end:

    use the paragraph name COMPONENT-NAME-END.

(b) Iteration

We use the COBOL IF and GO TO statements to implement the ITER construct, as indicated by the lines containing '!' — see figure 7.6.

```
G ITER UNTIL C3          G-ITER.                    !
  H SEQ                       IF CONDITION C3        !
     DO 11,12                    GO TO G-END.        !
     I ....                 H-SEQ.
       ::::                      OPERATION 11
     I END                       OPERATION 12
  H END                     I-.....
G END                            ::::
                           I-END.
                           H-END.
                                GO TO G-ITER.        !
                           G-END.                    !
```

Figure 7.6

The coding rules for an iteration are as follows.

1. At the start:

    use the paragraph name COMPONENT-NAME-ITER;
    use an IF statement with the ITER condition and true action GO TO
    COMPONENT-NAME-END.

2. At the end:

    use GO TO COMPONENT-NAME-ITER;
    use the paragraph name COMPONENT-NAME-END.

(c) Selection

Using the COBOL IF...THEN...ELSE and GO TO statements, as indicated by the lines containing '!', enables us to retain the structure of the schematic logic — see figure 7.7.

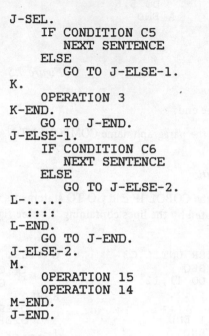

```
J SEL IF C5              J-SEL.                    !
  K                          IF CONDITION C5       !
    DO 3                         NEXT SENTENCE     !
  K END                      ELSE                  !
J ELSE 1 IF C6                   GO TO J-ELSE-1.   !
  L ....                  K.
    ::::                       OPERATION 3
  L END                  K-END.
J ELSE 2                     GO TO J-END.          !
  M                      J-ELSE-1.                 !
    DO 15,14                 IF CONDITION C6       !
  M END                        NEXT SENTENCE       !
J END                      ELSE                    !
                               GO TO J-ELSE-2.     !
                         L-.....
                             ::::
                         L-END.
                             GO TO J-END.          !
                         J-ELSE-2.                 !
                         M.
                             OPERATION 15
                             OPERATION 14
                         M-END.
                         J-END.                    !
```

Figure 7.7

The coding rules for a selection are as follows.

1. At the start:

> use the paragraph name COMPONENT-NAME-SEL;
> use an IF statement with the SEL condition,
> > true action NEXT SENTENCE
> > and false action GO TO COMPONENT-NAME-ELSE-1.

2. At ELSE n:

> use GO TO COMPONENT-NAME-END;
> use the paragraph name COMPONENT-NAME-ELSE-N;
> then provided it is not the last ELSE, use an IF statement with the ELSE n condition,
> > true action NEXT SENTENCE and
> > false action GO TO COMPONENT-NAME-ELSE-M (where M is N+1).

3. At the end:

    use the paragraph name COMPONENT-NAME-END.

There is an alternative which could equally well be used. All the

    'IF condition
        NEXT SENTENCE
    ELSE
        GO TO next else' statements

could be replaced by

    'IF not condition
        GO TO next else'.

The slight disadvantage of having to negate the appropriate condition is balanced by not having to use the ELSE part of the IF statement.

(d) Complete program

We shall now code a complete program (see figure 6.6 for schematic logic of the 'sales report' example) using the following approach.

1. Code the Identification Division, Environment Division and those parts of the Data Division required for input or output from the problem specification. For example

    01 AREA-HEADINGS.
       03 FILLER   PIC X(6)   VALUE "AREA".
       03 AREA-HD   PIC X.

2. From an inspection of the elementary operations and conditions, include in the Data Division any additional data items that will be required, such as STORED-YEAR.

3. Code the Procedure Division from the schematic logic, using the above rules for the control constructs and translating operations and conditions into COBOL. For example

    5.   Print area headings
        becomes
    MOVE IN-AREA TO AREA-HD
    WRITE PRINT-LINE FROM AREA-HEADINGS
    WRITE PRINT-LINE FROM SPACES AFTER 1.

As each operation or condition is coded:

(i) Check that appropriate data items have been included in the Data Division.

(ii) To prevent recoding of an operation or condition already used and to ensure that they are all coded, tick it off on the appropriate list.

As can be seen from the above example and the program in figure 7.8, an elementary operation may require more than one program statement.

```
00100       IDENTIFICATION DIVISION.
00200       PROGRAM-ID. SALES.
00300       ENVIRONMENT DIVISION.
00400       INPUT-OUTPUT SECTION.
00500       FILE-CONTROL.
00600           SELECT SALES-FILE ASSIGN TO DSK.
00700           SELECT OUTPUT-REPORT-FILE ASSIGN TO DSK.
00800       DATA DIVISION.
00900       FILE SECTION.
01000       FD  SALES-FILE
01100           RECORDING MODE IS ASCII
01200           VALUE OF ID "SALES SEQ".
01300       01  SALES-REC.
01400           03 IN-AREA            PIC X.
01500           03 IN-YEAR            PIC 99.
01600           03 IN-PRODUCT         PIC X(20).
01700           03 IN-AMOUNT          PIC 999.
01800       FD  OUTPUT-REPORT-FILE
01900           RECORDING MODE IS ASCII
02000           VALUE OF ID "SALES LPT".
02100       01  PRINT-LINE            PIC X(80).
02200       WORKING-STORAGE SECTION.
02300       01  AREA-HEADINGS.
02400           03 FILLER             PIC X(6)    VALUE "AREA".
02500           03 AREA-HD            PIC X.
02600       01  YEAR-TOTAL-LINE.
02700           03 FILLER             PIC X(12)   VALUE SPACES.
02800           03 FILLER             PIC X(11)   VALUE "YEAR TOTAL".
02900           03 YEAR-TOT           PIC ZZZZ9.
03000       01  AREA-TOTAL-LINE.
03100           03 FILLER             PIC X(12)   VALUE SPACES.
03200           03 FILLER             PIC X(11)   VALUE "AREA TOTAL".
03300           03 AREA-TOT           PIC ZZZZ9.
03400       01  DETAIL-LINE.
03500           03 OUT-PRODUCT        PIC X(25).
03600           03 OUT-AMOUNT         PIC ZZ9.
03700           03 FILLER             PIC XX      VALUE SPACES.
03800           03 OUT-RATING         PIC X(3).
03900       77  TOTAL-FOR-AREA        PIC 9(5).
04000       77  TOTAL-FOR-YEAR        PIC 9(5).
04100       77  STORED-AREA           PIC X.
04200       77  STORED-YEAR           PIC 99.
04300       PROCEDURE DIVISION.
04400       SALES-REPORT-SEQ.
04500           OPEN INPUT SALES-FILE OUTPUT OUTPUT-REPORT-FILE.
04600           READ SALES-FILE AT END
04700               MOVE HIGH-VALUES TO SALES-REC.
04800       REPORT-BODY-ITER.
04900           IF SALES-REC = HIGH-VALUES
05000               GO TO REPORT-BODY-END.
05100       PROCESS-AREA-SEQ.
05200       AREA-HEAD.
05300           MOVE IN-AREA TO AREA-HD
05400           WRITE PRINT-LINE FROM AREA-HEADINGS
05500           WRITE PRINT-LINE FROM SPACES AFTER 1.
05600           MOVE ZERO TO TOTAL-FOR-AREA.
05700           MOVE IN-AREA TO STORED-AREA.
05800       AREA-HEAD-END.
05900       AREA-BODY-ITER.
06000           IF SALES-REC = HIGH-VALUES
06100               OR IN-AREA NOT = STORED-AREA
```

Figure 7.8 (above and opposite)

```
06200          GO TO AREA-BODY-END.
06300   PROCESS-YEAR-SEQ.
06400       MOVE ZERO TO TOTAL-FOR-YEAR.
06500       MOVE IN-YEAR TO STORED-YEAR.
06600   YEAR-BODY-ITER.
06700       IF SALES-REC = HIGH-VALUES
06800          OR IN-AREA NOT = STORED-AREA
06900          OR IN-YEAR NOT = STORED-YEAR
07000          GO TO YEAR-BODY-END.
07100   RECORD-TO-LINE-SEQ.
07200   RECORD-TO-LINE-BODY-SEL.
07300       IF IN-AMOUNT < 100
07400          NEXT SENTENCE
07500       ELSE
07600          GO TO RECORD-TO-LINE-BODY-ELSE-1.
07700   SALES-UNDER-100.
07800       MOVE IN-PRODUCT TO OUT-PRODUCT
07900       MOVE IN-AMOUNT TO OUT-AMOUNT
08000       MOVE "!" TO OUT-RATING
08100       WRITE PRINT-LINE FROM DETAIL-LINE AFTER 1.
08200   SALES-UNDER-100-END.
08300       GO TO RECORD-TO-LINE-BODY-END.
08400   RECORD-TO-LINE-BODY-ELSE-1.
08500       IF IN-AMOUNT NOT > 300
08600          NEXT SENTENCE
08700       ELSE
08800          GO TO RECORD-TO-LINE-BODY-ELSE-2.
08900   SALES-100-TO-300.
09000       MOVE IN-PRODUCT TO OUT-PRODUCT
09100       MOVE IN-AMOUNT TO OUT-AMOUNT
09200       MOVE "!!" TO OUT-RATING
09300       WRITE PRINT-LINE FROM DETAIL-LINE AFTER 1.
09400   SALES-100-TO-300-END.
09500       GO TO RECORD-TO-LINE-BODY-END.
09600   RECORD-TO-LINE-BODY-ELSE-2.
09700   SALES-OVER-300.
09800       MOVE IN-PRODUCT TO OUT-PRODUCT
09900       MOVE IN-AMOUNT TO OUT-AMOUNT
10000       MOVE "!!!" TO OUT-RATING
10100       WRITE PRINT-LINE FROM DETAIL-LINE AFTER 1.
10200   SALES-OVER-300-END.
10300   RECORD-TO-LINE-BODY-END.
10400       ADD IN-AMOUNT TO TOTAL-FOR-AREA.
10500       ADD IN-AMOUNT TO TOTAL-FOR-YEAR.
10600       READ SALES-FILE AT END
10700              MOVE HIGH-VALUES TO SALES-REC.
10800   RECORD-TO-LINE-END.
10900       GO TO YEAR-BODY-ITER.
11000   YEAR-BODY-END.
11100   YEAR-TOTAL.
11200       MOVE TOTAL-FOR-YEAR TO YEAR-TOT
11300       WRITE PRINT-LINE FROM YEAR-TOTAL-LINE AFTER 2
11400       WRITE PRINT-LINE FROM SPACES AFTER 1.
11500   YEAR-TOTAL-END.
11600   PROCESS-YEAR-END.
11700       GO TO AREA-BODY-ITER.
11800   AREA-BODY-END.
11900   AREA-TOTAL.
12000       MOVE TOTAL-FOR-AREA TO AREA-TOT
12100       WRITE PRINT-LINE FROM AREA-TOTAL-LINE AFTER 2
12200       WRITE PRINT-LINE FROM SPACES AFTER 2.
12300   AREA-TOTAL-END.
12400   PROCESS-AREA-END.
12500       GO TO REPORT-BODY-ITER.
12600   REPORT-BODY-END.
12700       CLOSE SALES-FILE OUTPUT-REPORT-FILE.
12800       STOP RUN.
12900   SALES-REPORT-END.
```

7.4 BASIC as target language

In the examples and exercises, we have used long variable names (for example, AREA$) and integer variables (for example, YEARTOTAL%); these facilities are not available in all versions of BASIC.

Assuming a version of BASIC that provides a 'IF condition GOTO line number' statement, but does not possess a 'IF condition THEN statement(s) ELSE statement(s)' construct, the following examples illustrate how the structure of the schematic logic can be retained.

(a) Sequence and elementary component

The sequence parts are retained in the same order as they appear in the schematic logic — see figure 7.9.

```
A SEQ                   100   REM ** a seq **
  B                     110     REM ** b **
      DO 3,4            120       OPERATION 3
  B END                 130       OPERATION 4
  C ....                140     REM ** b end **
      ::::              150     REM ** c .... **
  C END                 :         ::::
      DO 5,6            200     REM ** c end **
A END                  210     OPERATION 5
                       220     OPERATION 6
                       230   REM ** a end **
```

Figure 7.9

The coding rules for a sequence or elementary component are as follows.

1. At the start:

   use the comment REM ** component name seq ** or REM ** component name **.

2. At the end:

   use the comment REM ** component name end **.

(b) Iteration

We use the 'IF condition GOTO line number' and 'GOTO line number' statements to code the ITER construct, as indicated by the lines containing '!' — see figure 7.10.

```
G ITER UNTIL C3        100   REM ** g iter **            !
   H SEQ               110      IF CONDITION C3 GOTO 300 !
      DO 11,12         120      REM ** h seq **
      I ....           130         OPERATION 11
       ::::            140         OPERATION 12
      I END            150         REM ** i .... **
   H END                :          ::::
G END                  270         REM ** i end **
                       280      REM ** h end **
                       290      GOTO 100                 !
                       300   REM ** g end **             !
```

Figure 7.10

The coding rules for an iteration are as follows.

1. At the start:

> use the comment REM ∗∗ component name iter ∗∗;
> use an IF statement with the ITER condition and true action
>   GOTO line no. of REM ∗∗ component name end ∗∗.

2. At the end:

> use GOTO line no. of REM ∗∗ component name iter ∗∗;
> use the comment REM ∗∗ component name end ∗∗.

(c) Selection

Using the 'IF condition GOTO line number' and 'GOTO line number' statements, as indicated by the lines containing '!', we can retain the structure of the schematic logic − see figure 7.11.

```
J SEL IF C5        100 REM ** j sel **                    !
   K               110    IF NOT (CONDITION C5) GOTO 160  !
      DO 3         120    REM ** k **
   K END           130       OPERATION 3
J ELSE 1 IF C2     140    REM ** k end **
   L ....          150    GOTO 310                         !
    ::::           160 REM ** j else 1 **                  !
   L END           170    IF NOT (CONDITION C2) GOTO 260   !
J ELSE 2           180    REM ** l .... **
   M                :        ::::
      DO 15,14     240    REM ** l end **
   M END           250    GOTO 310                         !
J END              260 REM ** j else 2 **                  !
                   270    REM ** m **
                   280       OPERATION 15
                   290       OPERATION 14
                   300    REM ** m end **
                   310 REM ** j end **                     !
```

Figure 7.11

```
100 REM ** sales report seq **
110    OPEN "SALESFILE.INP" FOR INPUT AS FILE #1
120    OPEN "REPFILE.OUT" FOR OUTPUT AS FILE #2
130    INPUT #1,AREA$,YEAR%,SALESPRODUCT$,SALESAMOUNT%
140    REM ** report body iter **
150      IF AREA$ = "Z" GOTO 700
160      REM ** process area seq **
170        REM ** area head **
180          PRINT #2,"AREA   ";AREA$
190          PRINT #2
200          AREATOTAL% = 0
210          STOREDAREA$ = AREA$
220        REM ** area head end **
230        REM ** area body iter **
240          IF AREA$ = "Z" OR AREA$ <> STOREDAREA$ GOTO 610
250          REM ** process year seq **
260            YEARTOTAL% = 0
270            STOREDYEAR% = YEAR%
280            REM ** year body iter **
290              IF AREA$ = "Z"
                     OR AREA$ <> STOREDAREA$
                     OR YEAR% <> STOREDYEAR% GOTO 530
300              REM ** record to line seq **
310              REM ** record to line body sel **
320                IF NOT (SALESAMOUNT% < 100) GOTO 370
330                REM ** sales under 100 **
340                  PRINT #2,SALESPRODUCT$;TAB(24);
                             SALESAMOUNT%;TAB(29);" !"
350                REM ** sales under 100 end **
360                  GOTO 470
370                REM ** record to line body else 1 **
380                IF NOT (SALESAMOUNT% <= 300) GOTO 430
390                REM ** sales 100 to 300 **
400                  PRINT #2,SALESPRODUCT$;TAB(24);
                             SALESAMOUNT%;TAB(29);" !!"
410                REM ** sales 100 to 300 end **
420                  GOTO 470
430                REM ** record to line body else 2 **
440                REM ** sales over 300 **
450                  PRINT #2,SALESPRODUCT$;TAB(24);
                             SALESAMOUNT%;TAB(29);" !!!"
460                REM ** sales over 300 end **
470              REM ** record to line body end **
480              AREATOTAL% = AREATOTAL% + SALESAMOUNT%
490              YEARTOTAL% = YEARTOTAL% + SALESAMOUNT%
500              INPUT #1,AREA$,YEAR%,SALESPRODUCT$,SALESAMOUNT%
510            REM ** record to line end **
520              GOTO 280
530          REM ** year body end **
540          REM ** year total **
550            PRINT #2
560            PRINT #2,TAB(12);"YEAR TOTAL";YEARTOTAL%
570            PRINT #2
580          REM ** year total end **
590        REM ** process year end **
600          GOTO 230
610        REM ** area body end **
620        REM ** area total **
630          PRINT #2
640          PRINT #2,TAB(12);"AREA TOTAL";AREATOTAL%
650          PRINT #2
660          PRINT #2
670        REM ** area total end **
680      REM ** process area end **
690        GOTO 140
700    REM ** report body end **
710    CLOSE #1,#2
720    STOP
730 REM ** sales report end **
```

Figure 7.12

The coding rules for a selection are as follows.

1. At the start:

> use the comment REM ** component name sel **;
> use an IF statement with the negation of the SEL condition and true action
> GOTO line no. of REM ** component name else 1 **.

2. At ELSE n:

> use GOTO line no. of REM ** component name end **;
> use REM ** component name else n **;
> then provided it is not the last ELSE, use an IF statement with the negation of the ELSE condition and true action
> GOTO line no. of REM ** component name else n+1 **.

3. At the end:

> use the comment REM ** component name end **.

(d) Complete program

We shall now code a complete program (see figure 6.6 for schematic logic of the 'sales report' example) using the following approach.

Code the program from the schematic logic using the above rules for the control constructs and translating operations and conditions into BASIC. For example

> 5. Print area headings
>
> becomes
>
> 180   PRINT #2,"AREA   ";AREA$
> 190   PRINT #2

As each operation or condition is coded, tick it off on the appropriate list to prevent recoding of an operation or condition already used and to ensure that all are eventually coded.

As can be seen from the above example and the program in figure 7.12, an elementary operation may require more than one program statement.

Note that the solution in figure 7.12 assumes that the last record on the input file is a dummy record (sentinel) with Z as the area code. End of file can then be detected by AREA$ = "Z".

7.5 Exercises

7.5.1. Code the program for exercise 4.3.1 in BASIC. The schematic logic is given in appendix A as solution 6.3.1. Assume that the final record in the production file contains a record type of 9 as an end of file indicator, and on output the count record precedes it.

The record layout for the production file is as follows:

RECTYPE%	record type	1 = ordinary record
		9 = end of file record
MACHINE$	machine description	
DATEPURCH$	date purchased	
REPDUE%	replacement indicator (9 if due).	

The layout for the count record is:

| RECTYPE% | record type | (=8) |
| REPCOUNT% | replacement count. | |

7.5.2. Code the program for exercise 4.3.2 in PASCAL. The schematic logic is given in appendix A as solution 6.3.2. Assume that the final record in the hospital file contains ZZZZ for ward as an end of file indicator. Use the type declarations shown in figure 7.13.

```
TYPE
    PACKED4 =               PACKED ARRAY [1..4] OF CHAR ;
    RECORDTYPE =
      RECORD
        WARD         : PACKED4 ;
        NAME         : PACKED ARRAY [1..20] OF CHAR ;
        PATIENT      : BOOLEAN ;
      END ;
```

Figure 7.13

7.5.3. Code the program for exercise 4.3.3 in COBOL. The schematic logic is given in appendix A as solution 6.3.3. Use the personnel record description given in figure 7.14.

```
01   PERSONNEL-REC.
       03 GRADE                PIC 999.
       03 NAME                 PIC X(17).
       03 O-LEVELS             PIC 9.
       03 A-LEVELS             PIC 9.
       03 DEGREE-Y-N           PIC X.
          88 HAS-DEGREE        VALUE "Y".
```

Figure 7.14

8 More Than One Input File

8.1 Merging data (at most, one record per key per file)

If we are to process more than one input file simultaneously, then very often the input files will have to be sorted into a specific order and, at the top level, will have very similar logical data structures.

One way of viewing such problems is that we must collate or merge the data from the input files in order to produce the required output. Such operations are done on the basis of matching key fields. Throughout this chapter, we assume that input files are sorted into ascending order of key value. At this stage we shall assume that there is, at most, one record per key per file.

The top level of the logical data structures for each input file in a collate or merge problem will inevitably indicate that the file is an iteration of each possible matching key — see figure 8.1.

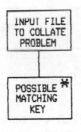

Figure 8.1

We use the term 'possible matching key' because each input file has the same set of allowable key values; so there is a potential for matching any key in one file with its corresponding key in another input file.

Further, each possible key may or may not be present in a particular file and is therefore a selection of either being present or absent. To illustrate this, consider two files containing records with unique keys — the range of possible key values being 1 to 4. The maximum number of possible records on each file is therefore 4. Let us say for file A that we have keys 1 and 3, and in file B that we have keys 2 and 3; that is

57

FILE A	FILE B
1	2
3	3

Clearly the presence or absence of a particular key value in a given file will have an effect on the collate process. Also the combinations of 'present' and 'absent' may indicate different processing actions (for example, if a record of a given key is present in file A only — copy the record to output; if present in both files — merge the data before output; if present in file B only — display an error message). The logical data structures for both files must therefore represent the following situation:

1 present or absent
2 present or absent
3 present or absent
4 present or absent

which gives the structure shown in figure 8.2.

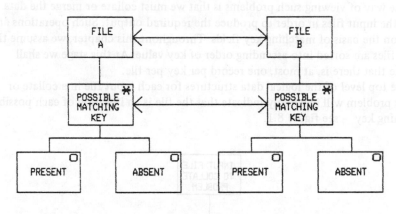

Figure 8.2

Notice that we did not regard FILE A as an iteration of KEY PRESENT ON A, nor FILE B as an iteration of KEY PRESENT ON B. Since these components do not correspond, we would not be able to combine the two input structures. So, how did we arrive at the above correspondences? The basic rule for more than one input file is that corresponding components must match. Clearly, FILE A and FILE B correspond. Since each file is an iteration of each possible key (1, 2, 3 and 4), the components POSSIBLE MATCHING KEY also correspond. As for the selection parts, file A key present does not necessarily match with file B key present, and similarly for the other selection parts.

If we refer back to the simple key range of 1 to 4 only, there are obviously four combinations of 'PRESENT and ABSENT'. These combinations must be shown on the merged input structure. We combine the data structures as shown in figure 8.3.

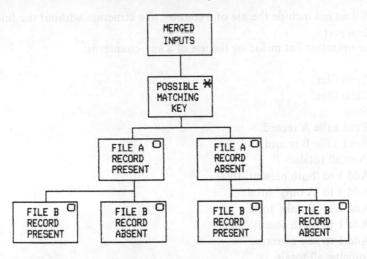

Figure 8.3

This can be simplified by regarding the selection POSSIBLE MATCHING KEY as having four component parts, as shown in figure 8.4.

Further examination of the problem indicates that the fourth selection part, 'file A record absent and file B record absent', is detectable only if we process every possible key value (for example, by means of a key counter). If we are processing only those keys that occur in the input files, then this selection part does not appear on the combined input structure.

We can illustrate the difference in the two cases by solving the problem of counting the number of key values for each of the conditions. The output for such a problem is trivial, so our combined input structure becomes the program structure and we can proceed to allocate operations (which include the use of a key counter) to it. After we have solved this problem, we shall apply an operation list

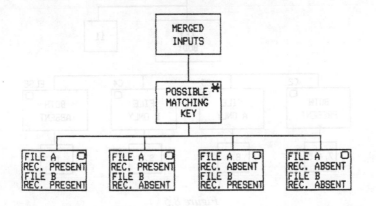

Figure 8.4

which does not include the use of a counter to a structure without the final selection part.

The operation list including the use of a key counter is:

1. Open files.
2. Close files.
3. Stop.
4. Read a file A record.
5. Read a file B record.
6. Print all totals.
7. Add 1 to 'both present' total.
8. Add 1 to 'A only' total.
9. Add 1 to 'B only' total.
10. Add 1 to 'both absent' total.
11. Add 1 to key counter.
12. Initialise all totals.
13. Initialise key counter = 1.

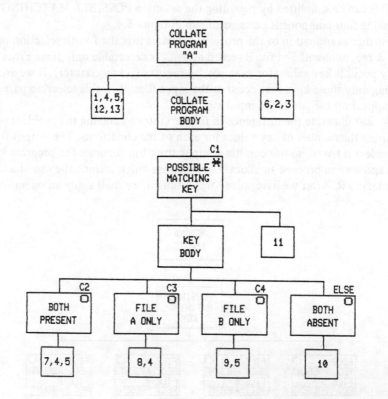

Figure 8.5

Allocating these to the program structure and including body boxes, as required, gives the structure shown in figure 8.5 for the COLLATE PROBLEM WITH ALL POSSIBLE KEYS PROCESSED.

The condition list for this problem is:

C1 — Until end of key range (key counter > maximum).
C2 — If key counter = A key = B key.
C3 — If key counter = A key < > B key.
C4 — If key counter = B key < > A key.

Note that the conditions C2, C3 and C4 will be affected by the way in which the target language handles end of file. For example, C3 in full should allow for the cases where end of file has been reached. That is

C3 — If (key counter = A key and not end of file A)
       and (key counter < > B key or end of file B).

If, however, the key of each file is set to an impossibly high value when end of file is reached, then whenever end of file B is true, so is key counter < > B key; similarly, key counter = A key will ensure that we are not at the end of file A. Henceforth, we shall assume that end of file is handled in this way and use the above simplified versions of C2, C3 and C4.

Now let us turn our attention to the problem where we are interested in only the keys for which records are present in one or both input files. In this case, the data structures of figure 8.2 are combined to give a merged input structure which, assuming that only the appropriate totals are output, becomes the program structure — COLLATE PROBLEM WITH ONLY THOSE KEYS PRESENT ON ONE OR BOTH OF THE INPUT FILES PROCESSED — see figure 8.6.

For this problem we have a different condition list and, of course, do not need operations 10, 11 and 13 from the operation list.

C1 — Until end of both files
C2 — If A key = B key.
C3 — If A key < B key.

One further case, which follows from the above discussion, occurs when we are required to process records from one file only (file A) but take into account any data that may be present for corresponding keys in another file (file B). In other words, we are interested in only two of the collate possibilities:

file A record present and file B record present;
file A record present and file B record absent.

Assuming that there are key values satisfying 'file A record absent and file B record present', but we are not interested in counting them, and that file B is a sequential file, then the program structure is the same as the previous example. We still need to read past the unwanted records in file B, but we do not need operation 9.

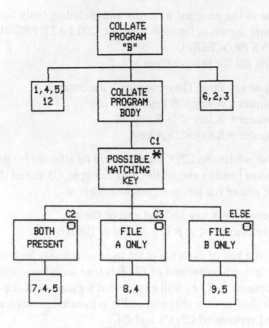

Figure 8.6

However, as we want to access only those records in file B that are also in file A, we can make file B a direct access file. The 'read a file B record' operation (number 5 in our list) then becomes:

5. Attempt to read file B record with key = A key.

In this case the data structures of figure 8.2 are combined to give a merged input structure which, assuming that only appropriate totals are output, becomes the program structure – COLLATE PROBLEM WITH ONLY THOSE KEYS PRESENT ON ONE OF THE INPUT FILES PROCESSED – see figure 8.7.

Note that figure 8.7 needs only operations 1 to 8 and 12 (9 to 11 and 13 from the original list are obviously not required) and has only two conditions:

C1 – Until end of file A.
C2 – If record found in direct access file B.

In the above examples, we have virtually ignored the influence of output files so that we could concentrate on the merging of input files. Let us now consider a collate example with a simple output file.

In a payroll system, two sequential files are used: a wages file for weekly paid employees and a salaries file for monthly paid employees. Both files are sorted by employee number. An employee should not be present in both files, but it is thought that this might have occurred owing to clerical errors. It is therefore required to produce a report with headings, the details of any employees who are on both files, and then totals of the number of records in each file.

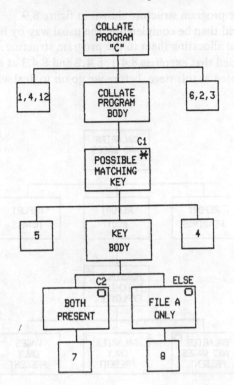

Figure 8.7

Having drawn the data structures for both input files (see figure 8.2) and the output file, first we combine the input files and then draw correspondences between the output and the combined input, as shown in figure 8.8.

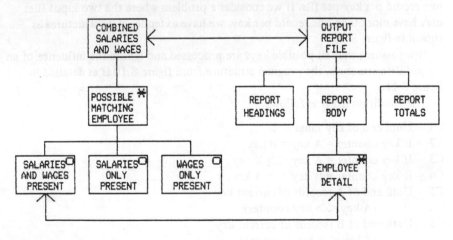

Figure 8.8

This gives us the program structure shown in figure 8.9.

The design would then be completed in the usual way by listing the operations and conditions, and allocating them to the program structure.

It is recommended that exercises 8.4.1, 8.4.2 and 8.4.3 at the end of this chapter are attempted at this stage, before we go on to deal with more complex problems.

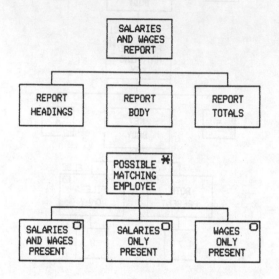

Figure 8.9

8.2 More complex merges (more than one record per key)

The solutions given above really apply only to the cases where there is, at most, one record per key per file. If we consider a problem where the two input files may have more than one record per key, we have extended data structures as shown in figure 8.10.

If we assume that all possible keys are processed and ignore the influence of an output data structure, the program structure from figure 8.10 is as detailed in figure 8.11.

The condition list is as follows:

C1 – Until end of key range.
C2 – If key counter = A key = B key.
C3 – If key counter = A key $<>$ B key.
C4 – If key counter = B key $<>$ A key.
C5 – Until end of A records of current key
        (A key $<>$ key counter).
C6 – Until end of B records of current key
        (B key $<>$ key counter).

As in the previous (?) file, we have described the structure by repeating POSSIBLE MATCHING KEY a number of times as necessary.

BOTH PRESENT shows a sequence of A RECORD BODY followed by B RECORD BODY. Because in addition to A RECORD within the FILE A the structure and the inclusion of B RECORD now and the B file data structure that ...

Given the ... list of copying all records ... definition of B file-d ... If the A ... copying to the ... in the ... file ... every A ... key is present on one or both files ... processed. The data structure ... a file to the con-... that to all ... it continues to ... will also ...

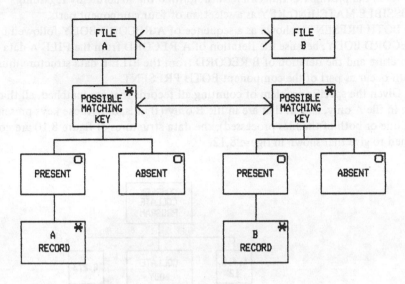

Figure 8.10

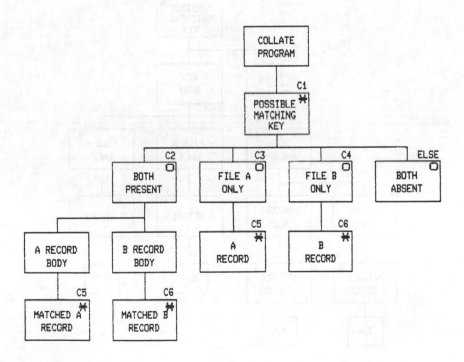

Figure 8.11

As in the previous section, we have simplified the structure by regarding POSSIBLE MATCHING KEY as a selection of four component parts.

BOTH PRESENT is shown as a sequence of A RECORD BODY followed by B RECORD BODY, because the iteration of A RECORD from the FILE A data structure and the iteration of B RECORD from the FILE B data structure must both occur as part of the component BOTH PRESENT.

Given the specific problem of counting all records that are matched, all that are in file A only, and all that are in file B only (that is, only those keys present on one or both of the files processed), the data structures of figure 8.10 are combined to give that shown in figure 8.12.

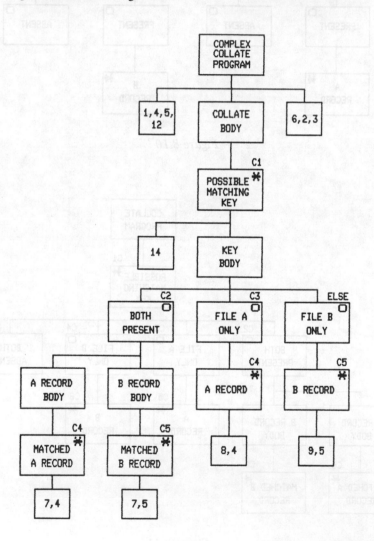

Figure 8.12

The condition list for this is:

C1 — Until end of both input files.
C2 — If A key = B key.
C3 — If A key < B key.
C4 — Until change of key (A key <> stored key).
C5 — Until change of key (B key <> stored key).

An additional operation to those used in the previous section is necessary in order to implement C4 and C5:

14. Store key (the lower of A and B).

8.3 The sequential file update

We can apply the collate problem solution to the sequential file update problem. Assuming, at most, one record per key per file, the data structures of an input and output master file and a transaction file are as shown in figure 8.13.

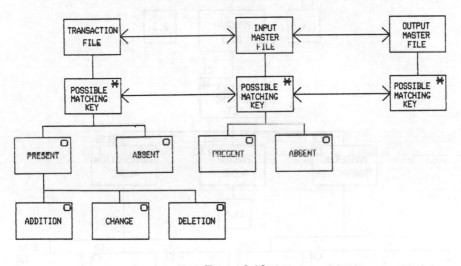

Figure 8.13

By combining the data structures, as we did in section 8.1, and noting that we are not interested in the condition 'transaction file record absent and input master record absent', we arrive at the program structure shown in figure 8.14.

The allocated conditions and operations are:

C1 — Until end of both input files.
C2 — If master key = transaction key.
C3 — If master key < transaction key.

C4 — If transaction type = 'addition'.
C5 — If transaction type = 'change'.

1. Open files.
2. Close files.
3. Stop.
4. Read a master record.
5. Read a transaction record.
6. Write a new master record.
7. Change an existing record and write to output.
8. Display 'error – addition for existing record'.
9. Display 'error – delete for non-existent record'.
10. Display 'error – change for non-existent record'.
11. Write unchanged master record to output.

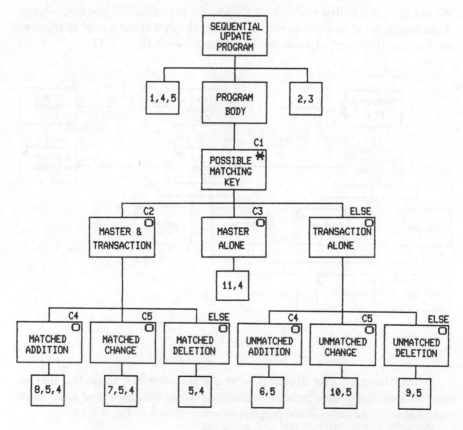

Figure 8.14

Notice how the components of the transaction file that are part of PRESENT are repeated in the program structure for each of the selection parts that include 'transaction present'.

The above example demonstrates the principles of the sequential file update when there is, at most, one transaction per master file record. Let us now consider a problem where there is more than one transaction record for a given key.

In a simple stock control system, a sequential master file is maintained with one record for each product in stock. The products are identified by a stock number. A transaction file is applied to the master file at the end of each day and a new carried forward master file is produced. The transaction file records are of two types: (a) change the description of the product; and (b) change the quantity. There may be more than one transaction record for any given stock number. An error message is displayed for each transaction record without a corresponding master file record. The data structures for this problem are given in figure 8.15.

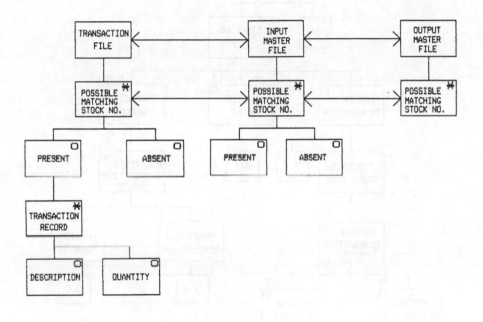

Figure 8.15

Combining at the points of correspondence and remembering the principles from our previous examples gives us the program structure of figure 8.16, to which we have added appropriate operations and conditions.

The conditions and operations for figure 8.16 are:

C1 — Until end of both input files.
C2 — If master stock number = transaction stock number.
C3 — If master stock number < transaction stock number.
C4 — Until change of transaction stock number.
C5 — If transaction type = change of description.

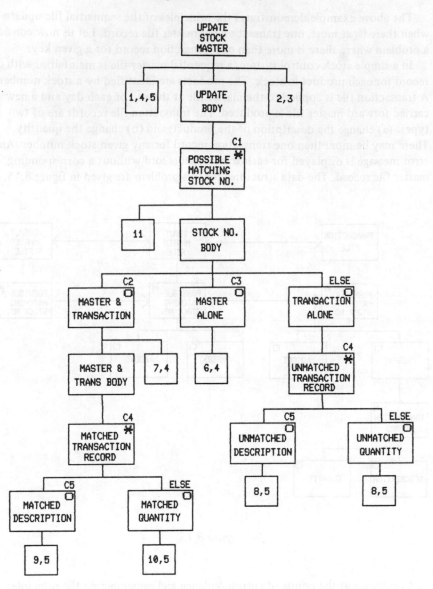

Figure 8.16

1. Open files.
2. Close files.
3. Stop.
4. Read a master file record.
5. Read a transaction file record.
6. Write unchanged master record to output.

7. Write amended master record to output.
8. Display 'transaction alone' error message.
9. Change master file record description.
10. Change master file record quantity.
11. Store transaction stock number.

Note that the components UNMATCHED DESCRIPTION and UNMATCHED QUANTITY have the same allocated operations. One could optimise this by removing these components and making UNMATCHED TRANSACTION RECORD an elementary component with the allocated operations 8 and 5. Optimisation of this kind will simplify the structure, but it will also make it more difficult to amend. For instance, if we were later required to display a particular error message for an unmatched description transaction, we would have to restore the components that we removed.

Of course, many sequential file updates are more complex than the above, essentially because of the complexity of the transaction file. For instance, a realistic transaction file would be sorted so that for any key the addition(s) come before the change(s) which come before the deletion(s). Also, second and subsequent additions and deletions for any key would give rise to an error.

We conclude this chapter with the data structure for such a transaction file — see figure 8.17.

8.4 Exercises

For each of the first three exercises you should:

(a) Produce logical data structures for the input files, identical to figure 8.2 (though you should use component names appropriate to the problem), together with an output file structure.
(b) Combine the input data structures to produce a merged input structure with selection parts appropriate to the problem; then combine this structure with the output structure to produce a program structure.
(c) List conditions and elementary operations, then allocate them to the program structure, incorporating 'body' boxes as necessary.

You may assume in all cases that the files are appropriately sorted.

8.4.1. A large used car sales organisation keeps a direct access file containing records of each car that it has for sale. Included in the records are registration number, manufacturer and model. A second file is built up as cars are sold — the records in this file contain only registration number and date sold. Once weekly, the files are used to produce a list of descriptions (that is, manufacturer and model) of cars sold. Occasionally, there is a sale recorded without a corresponding description record being available, in which case 'description not known' is printed.

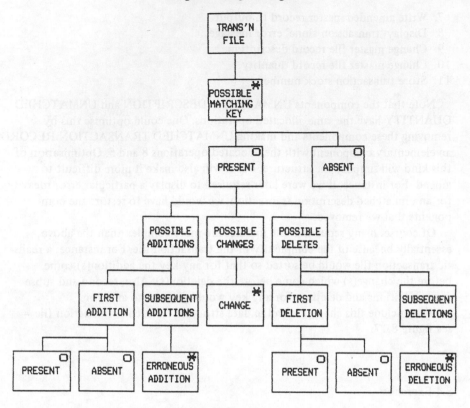

Figure 8.17

8.4.2. Two files are kept by Computa Training Limited. The first contains the names of all students who have been entered by Computa Training for the COBOL proficiency exam. The second contains the names of all students who have passed the exam. Not all students pass the exam and some may have been recorded as passed without being recorded as entered. It is required to produce an error report of those in this latter category, followed by the percentage pass rate of the correct records.

8.4.3. A C.A.L. program for infants requires them to match each of a list of 26 words (each beginning with a different letter) with a set of 26 pictures. The pictures are flashed onto a VDU screen and the infant has 20 seconds to make the match. When the match is made, the picture is deleted from the picture file and the word from the word list file. The initial letter of the word is used as the key in each file. After 30 minutes the session is over, and this leaves a number of picture records (which incidentally contain graphics details and the word that the picture represents) in one file, and a number of word records in another. The number of records in each should be the same but, owing to a software bug, they are not. To help the

software design team to find the bug, you are required to produce the
following:

(i)   a list of initial letters of the words that have been deleted from both
      files, followed by
(ii) the percentage of picture file records remaining, followed by
(iii) the percentage of word file records remaining, followed by
(iv) the number of words with corresponding pictures that remain in the
      files.

8.4.4. A library records the following data when a book is borrowed, returned
or renewed:

- borrower's reference number (6 digits)
- the date (dd mm yy)
- the book catalogue number (8 chars)
- a code = 1 for loan; 2 for renewal; 3 for return
- the time (hh mm ss).

At the end of each day the data collected are sorted into ascending
order of time of day within catalogue number. The sorted file is then used
to update a sequential book master file containing records as follows:

- book catalogue number (the sort key)
- date
- by whom borrowed (reference) if applicable.

If the transaction code = 1, the date and the borrower's reference are
changed in the master file record. If the transaction code = 2, the date only
is changed. If the transaction code = 3, the borrower's reference in the
master file is filled with spaces. There may be more than one transaction
per book.

The only error situation to be considered is when a transaction record
does not match a master record. This should be reported by a simple
displayed message.

You are required to design a program to update the book status master
file. Go through each stage from logical data structures to a program
structure with allocated operations and conditions.

9 Structure Clashes and Inversion

9.1 Types of structure clash

We briefly mentioned the idea of structure clashes at the end of chapter 4. Structure clashes occur when it is not possible to combine logical data structures to produce a single program structure, because the logical data structures contradict or clash with each other.

There are, in fact, three different types of structure clash to consider — and resolve:

(a) ordering clash
(b) boundary clash
(c) interleaving clash.

9.2 Ordering clash

A company keeps an expenditure file sorted by department. If it was required to produce a list of all items costing more than £100 in ascending order of cost, irrespective of department, we would create the data structures shown in figure 9.1.

Since the number of items per department is not equal to the number of high cost items on the list file, we cannot draw a correspondence between ITEM and HIGH COST ITEM. Although the set of items represented by HIGH COST is identical to the set of items represented by HIGH COST ITEM, the items are not in the same order and hence we cannot draw a correspondence between them. Consequently, we cannot combine the structures to produce a program structure.

However, we could resolve the clash by sorting the expenditure file into strict order of item cost only, as shown in figure 9.2.

9.3 Boundary clash

9.3.1 Why boundary clashes occur

Suppose we are to produce a print program in which variable length blocks of information are to be printed about cars, one for each model in a car details file.

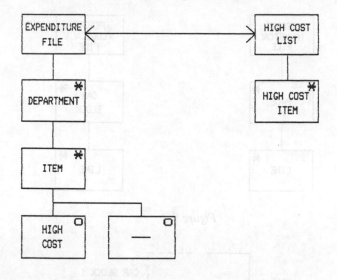

Figure 9.1

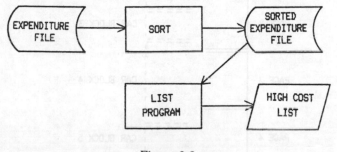

Figure 9.2

Each block has a car make and model, followed by a variable number of print lines. The pages are to be numbered, and the car make and model are to be repeated at the head of a page when a block is split over more than one page. The print file has effectively two structures: the structure of the physical medium on which it is written (the printed page), and the structure of the data to be written (the grouping of lines by car model). Both of these structures must be taken into account. But, ignoring headings for the sake of simplicity, this gives us the situation shown in figure 9.3.

The difficulty is that a car model may be entirely contained within one page or may be split between pages — see figure 9.4.

Obviously we cannot draw a correspondence between PAGE and CAR BLOCK. Furthermore, we cannot regard PAGE as an iteration of CAR BLOCK, or CAR BLOCK as an iteration of PAGE. Neither represents the relationship between pages and car blocks, since the boundary of a page clashes with the boundary of a car block.

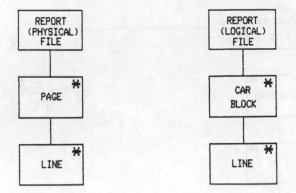

Figure 9.3

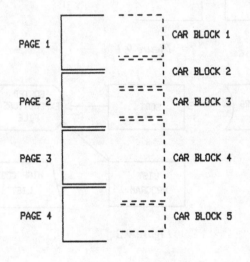

Figure 9.4

9.3.2 A typical example

A student file contains marks sorted by course. We are required to produce a
report which is split into pages, with a heading on each page. Student names and
marks are to be listed with totals at the end of each course. There is no relationship between course and page. We could have a number of courses per page (and
several total lines) or a course could be spread over a number of pages. We cannot
ignore the division of the input file into courses (because we are to produce totals
at the end of each course), and we cannot ignore the division of the output file
into pages (because we are to produce headings at the beginning of each page).

The appropriate data structures are shown in figure 9.5.

Obviously STUDENT FILE corresponds with REPORT FILE and STUDENT
MARK corresponds with DETAIL. But, COURSE does not correspond with

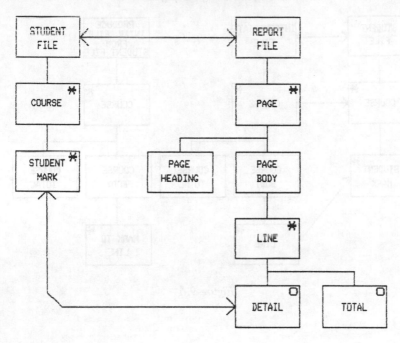

Figure 9.5

PAGE and we cannot regard one as an iteration of the other. The boundary of COURSE clashes with the boundary of PAGE. Clearly we are not going to be able to combine them to produce a program structure. However, there is a solution to the problem.

9.4 Solving the boundary clash

First, notice how we overcame the ordering clash (figure 9.2). In creating the intermediate file, SORTED EXPENDITURE FILE, we have, in effect, solved two simpler problems. We can use a similar approach when faced with the more difficult problem of a boundary clash.

Consider the student marks problem above. There would be no difficulty in creating a program to read the student file and simply to produce detail lines of print and, at appropriate points, course totals (that is, we have avoided the complication of page boundaries).

The data structures and resultant program structure are given in figure 9.6.

Similarly, if we had an intermediate print file consisting simply of lines of print (detail lines interspersed at appropriate points by total lines), we would have little difficulty in producing the report file complete with page headings from it. The data structures are shown in figure 9.7.

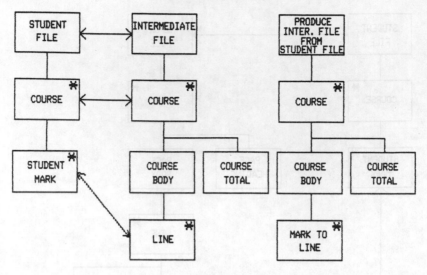

Figure 9.6

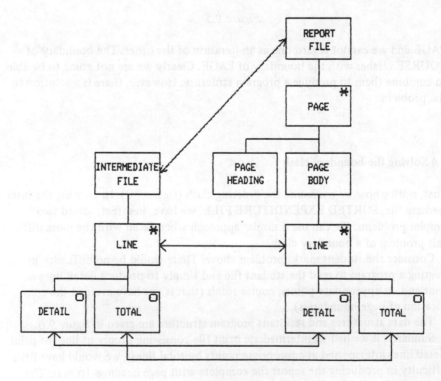

Figure 9.7

These give the program structure shown in figure 9.8.

So, we have solved two smaller problems and we can connect them as shown in figure 9.9.

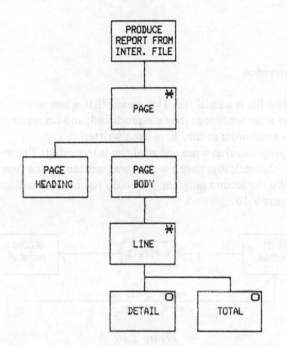

Figure 9.8

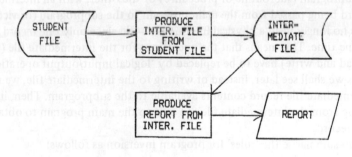

Figure 9.9

Because we have both to write to and read from the intermediate file, perhaps this is not the most efficient solution from a processing point of view. But, the structures that we have produced are correct and maintainable, and there is a technique called program inversion which gets rid of the need for the intermediate file.

Obviously, there is only one physical intermediate file. However, as this example illustrates, the logical data structures for this file may vary, depending on whether it is viewed as the output (as in the first program) or the input (as in the second program).

9.5 Program inversion

The intermediate file is a serial file. This means that when writing, the records are written one after another as they are produced; and on reading, the records are read in the same order as they have been written.

If the two programs that write and read the intermediate file were executed at the same time, theoretically, once a record was written by the first program, it could be read by the second program. We could represent this diagrammatically as shown in figure 9.10.

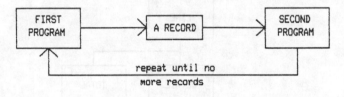

Figure 9.10

A practical method of achieving this is to combine the two programs by making one a subprogram (subroutine or procedure) of the other, with an intermediate file record being passed from the main program to the subprogram (or vice versa). Thus we no longer need a physical intermediate file since only one record is active at any one time. This means that the operations for the intermediate file (open, close, read and write) have to be replaced by 'logical input/output operations'. In effect, as we shall see later, instead of writing to the intermediate file, we make the intermediate file record contents available to the subprogram. Then, instead of reading from the intermediate file, we exit to the main program to obtain another record.

We can summarise the 'rules' for program inversion as follows:

1. Design the two programs independently up to and including the schematic logic stage.
2. Decide on the most appropriate inversion (that is, which program should be the subprogram).
3. Identify the input/output (I/O) operations for the intermediate file as 'logical I/O operations'.
4. Apply specific rules for the implementation of the 'logical I/O operations' at the coding stage.

The way in which we remove the intermediate file and make one program a subprogram called by the other is now demonstrated in detail. Let us apply the technique to our student marks boundary clash problem (figure 9.9). The two program structures are given in figures 9.6 and 9.8. For each program, we allocate operations and conditions and then produce schematic logic.

Program 1 – produce an intermediate file from the student file (see figure 9.11)

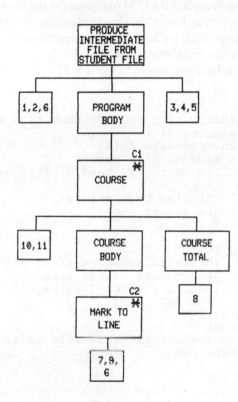

Figure 9.11

The condition list is:

C1 – Until end of student file.
C2 – Until change of course or end of student file.

The operation list is:

1. Open student file.
2. Open intermediate file.
3. Close student file.
4. Close intermediate file.
5. Stop.

6. Read a student file record.
7. Write intermediate file detail record.
8. Write intermediate file total record.
9. Accumulate course total.
10. Initialise course total.
11. Store course code.

Since we are going to replace the I/O operations for the intermediate file by
'logical I/O operations', they have to be clearly identified. Therefore, instead of
just one operation 'open files', we have used two separate operations for student
file and intermediate file, and similarly for 'close files'.

Now the schematic logic is as shown in figure 9.12.

```
PRODUCE INTERMEDIATE FILE FROM STUDENT FILE SEQ   [Program 1
    DO 1   [Open student file
    DO 2   [Open intermediate file
    DO 6   [Read a student file record
    PROGRAM BODY ITER UNTIL C1   [end of student file
        COURSE SEQ
            DO 10   [Initialise course total
            DO 11   [Store course code
            COURSE BODY ITER UNTIL C2   [change of course
                                          or end of student file
                MARK TO LINE
                    DO 7   [Write intermediate file detail record
                    DO 9   [Accumulate course total
                    DO 6   [Read a student file record
                MARK TO LINE END
            COURSE BODY END
            COURSE TOTAL
                DO 8   [Write intermediate file total record
            COURSE TOTAL END
        COURSE END
    PROGRAM BODY END
    DO 3   [Close student file
    DO 4   [Close intermediate file
    DO 5   [Stop
PRODUCE INTERMEDIATE FILE FROM STUDENT FILE END
```

Figure 9.12

Program 2 – produce report file from the intermediate file (see figure 9.13)

The condition list is:

C3 – Until end of intermediate file.
C4 – Until end of page or end of intermediate file.
C5 – If a detail line.

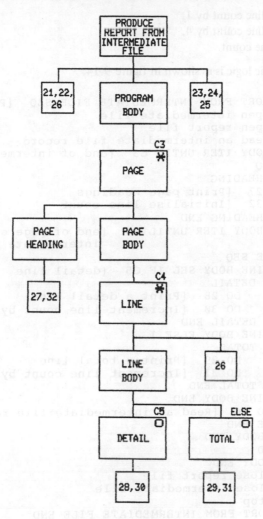

Figure 9.13

The operation list is:

21. Open intermediate file.
22. Open report file.
23. Close report file.
24. Close intermediate file.
25. Stop.
26. Read an intermediate file record.
27. Print page headings.
28. Print a detail line.
29. Print a total line.

30. Increment line count by 1.
31. Increment line count by 4.
32. Initialise line count.

The schematic logic is as shown in figure 9.14.

```
PRODUCE REPORT FROM INTERMEDIATE FILE SEQ    [Program 2
    DO 21   [Open intermediate file
    DO 22   [Open report file
    DO 26   [Read an intermediate file record
    PROGRAM BODY ITER UNTIL C3   [end of intermediate file
        PAGE SEQ
            PAGE HEADING
                DO 27   [Print page headings
                DO 32   [Initialise line count
            PAGE HEADING END
            PAGE BODY ITER UNTIL C4    [end of page or end of
                                        intermediate file
                LINE SEQ
                    LINE BODY SEL IF C5   [detail line
                        DETAIL
                            DO 28   [Print a detail line
                            DO 30   [Increment line count by 1
                        DETAIL END
                    LINE BODY ELSE 1
                        TOTAL
                            DO 29   [Print a total line
                            DO 31   [Increment line count by 4
                        TOTAL END
                    LINE BODY END
                    DO 26   [Read an intermediate file record
                LINE END
            PAGE BODY END
        PAGE END
    PROGRAM BODY END
    DO 23   [Close report file
    DO 24   [Close intermediate file
    DO 25   [Stop
PRODUCE REPORT FROM INTERMEDIATE FILE END
```

Figure 9.14

Now we will choose to make the second program a subroutine of the first. Coding from the schematic logic may now be done with specific rules for the identified 'logical I/O operations'.

First, the main program (program 1). Instead of writing to the intermediate file, we are going to call the subroutine and pass an intermediate file record together with an intermediate file status indicator, which indicates when the file is open or closed (in order to implement 'end of intermediate file' for conditions C3 and C4).

We code

2. Open intermediate file

by initialising an intermediate file status indicator.
In COBOL:

    MOVE 0 TO INTER-EOF.

In PASCAL:

    INTEREOF := FALSE ;

In BASIC:

    100 INTER = 0

We code

7. Write intermediate file detail record

by calling the subroutine and making available the intermediate file record and the intermediate file status indicator. The type of intermediate file record (detail or total) must also be conveyed to the subroutine. For illustrative purposes, we will make these available by parameter passing in COBOL and using global areas in PASCAL and BASIC.
In COBOL:

    MOVE "D" TO D-REC-TYPE.
    MOVE COURSE-CODE TO D-COURSE.
    MOVE NAME TO D-NAME.
    MOVE MARK TO D-MARK.
    CALL REP-SR USING INTER-EOF DETAIL-RECORD.

In PASCAL:

    RECTYPE := 'D' ,
    REPORTSR ;

In BASIC:

    1000 PA$ = "D": REM indicate detail line
    1100 GOSUB 2300: REM print subroutine

We code

8. Write intermediate file total record

by calling the subprogram as above.
In COBOL:

    MOVE "T" TO T-REC-TYPE.
    MOVE STORED-COURSE TO T-COURSE.
    MOVE COURSE-TOT TO T-TOTAL.
    CALL REP-SR USING INTER-EOF TOTAL-RECORD.

In PASCAL:

```
RECTYPE := 'T' ;
REPORTSR ;
```

In BASIC:

```
1400 PA$ = "T": REM indicate total line
1500 GOSUB 2300: REM print subroutine
```

We code

4. Close intermediate file

by calling the subprogram as above, except that the intermediate file status indicator is set to 'end of file' and the intermediate file record contents are irrelevant. In COBOL:

```
MOVE 1 TO INTER-EOF.
CALL REP-SR USING INTER-EOF NULL-RECORD.
```

In PASCAL:

```
INTEREOF := TRUE ;
REPORTSR ;
```

In BASIC:

```
1800 INTER = 1
1900 GOSUB 2300: REM print subroutine
```

Now the coding for the subprogram (program 2). For a 'logical read' of the intermediate file we exit to the main program to obtain an intermediate file record. In order to maintain continuity within the subprogram, on re-entry, we must ensure that the subprogram is executed from the instruction after the appropriate 'read'. This means inserting labels at each point of exit; and right at the beginning of the subprogram, including a statement which will transfer control to the point in the code from where we last exited.
In COBOL:

```
GO TO ENTRY-1 ENTRY-2...ENTRY-n
    DEPENDING ON ENTRY-STATUS.
ENTRY-1.
```

There will be the same number of ENTRY-n labels as read intermediate file statements (that is, 2 in our case). ENTRY-STATUS is a WORKING-STORAGE entry in the subprogram, with an initial value of one.
In PASCAL:

```
IF ENTRYSTATUS = 1 THEN GOTO 10
ELSE IF ENTRYSTATUS = 2 THEN GOTO 20
ELSE IF ENTRYSTATUS = n THEN GOTO n0 ;
10:
```

where 10, 20, n0 are declared as labels. ENTRYSTATUS is an integer variable
initialised to 1 at the start of the main program.
In BASIC:

```
2400 IF ES% = 1 THEN 2700: REM entry point 1
2500 IF ES% = 2 THEN 3600: REM entry point 2
2600 IF ES% = n THEN mmmm: REM entry point n
```

where ES% (the entry status) is initialised to 1 at the start of the main program.
   We code

21. Open intermediate file
    and the first occurrence of
26. Read an intermediate file record

by nothing!! This is because the first call of the subroutine passes the first intermediate file record.

   We code the second and subsequent occurrences of

26. Read an intermediate file record

by setting the entry status indicator to a value that indicates which occurrence of
the 'read' it is (that is, for the second read use value 2, for the third use 3 etc.);
then by exiting from the subprogram (or passing control to a common exit point);
then by inserting a label to correspond to the entry point handling code mentioned
above.
In COBOL:

```
        MOVE 2 TO ENTRY-STATUS.
        EXIT PROGRAM.
    ENTRY-2.
```

In PASCAL:

```
        ENTRYSTATUS := 2 ;
        GOTO 9999 ;
    20:
```

where the label 9999 is situated as a common exit point from the subprogram
(procedure).
In BASIC:

```
3400 ES% = 2
3500 RETURN
3600 REM entry point 2
```

   We code

24. Close intermediate file

by nothing!!
   We replace

25. Stop

by code to exit from the subprogram.
In COBOL:

EXIT PROGRAM.

In PASCAL, this is not applicable.
In BASIC:

5000 RETURN

We code

end of intermediate file in C3 and C4

by testing the value of the intermediate file status indicator.

A full implementation of this boundary clash solution is given in each of the three languages in appendix J.

The coding rules given above are now summarised in figure 9.15. You may find

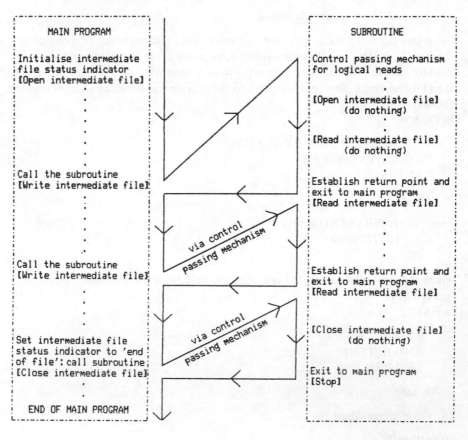

Figure 9.15

it beneficial to re-examine the rules in the light of this diagram.

In the above example we overcame the structure clash by creating an intermediate file of LINES (that is, using one LINE per intermediate file record). There was no point in using a record larger than LINE (such as PAGE), since that would not remove the clash. If the clashing logical data structures had contained an entity smaller than LINE (for example, FIELD or CHARACTER) in addition to LINE, then creating an intermediate file of this entity would have removed the clash, but such a process would obviously be inefficient. In general, we create an intermediate file of the largest entity common to the clashing structures (that is, the highest level non-clashing component).

We have explained the technique of inversion by providing coding rules that can be applied directly to the schematic logic of the two programs. However, when developing such programs, it is recommended that you initially code the two programs separately (that is, without using subprograms); test program 1 to create the intermediate file, then test program 2 using this intermediate file as input; then, once the two programs are correct, apply the coding rules to remove the intermediate file by making program 2 a subprogram of program 1.

As exercises 9.7.1 and 9.7.2 relate to the boundary clash and program inversion, you may attempt them at this stage, before considering the interleaving clash.

9.6 Interleaving clash

Consider a multiprogramming computer which runs a number of jobs (each containing a number of programs) simultaneously. We could show the schedule with a simple bar chart like that shown in figure 9.16.

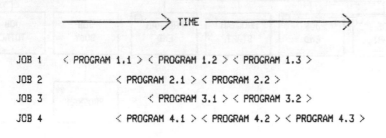

Figure 9.16

Suppose the computer logged the start and finish of the jobs and the programs, then the data would be as shown in figure 9.17.

If we attempt to process the data (log file) to produce details of elapsed time per job and per program, we find that the structure of the log file just does not represent job or program entities. The entities we want are interleaved; the only way we can draw a logical data structure is to show that the logging file records

```
JOB 1          START    9.00
PROGRAM 1.1    START    9.00
JOB 2          START   10.00
PROGRAM 2.1    START   10.00
JOB 4          START   10.00
PROGRAM 4.1    START   10.00
PROGRAM 1.1    END     10.30
PROGRAM 1.2    START   10.30
JOB 3          START   10.30
PROGRAM 3.1    START   10.30
PROGRAM 2.1    END     11.30
PROGRAM 2.2    START   11.30
```

etc.....etc.

Figure 9.17

are either job starts, job ends, program starts or program ends. So, we have the structures given in figure 9.18.

The structure clash is clear. LOG FILE corresponds with LOG ANALYSIS, but further correspondences are impossible.

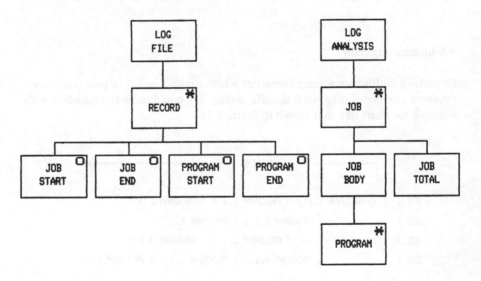

Figure 9.18

One solution is perhaps obvious — if we sort the log file into program within job order, we have no problems. But what if there is no time to sort or if we want a continuous analysis throughout the day? We must apply another solution.

Program inversion can be applied to solve the problem. Essentially, the solution is the same as that outlined for the boundary clash problem above, except that we have more than one intermediate file (that is, one per job). The first program simply creates a new file for each new job and writes each record from the log file to the appropriate job file. The second program reads each job file in turn and produces the analysis. Of course, it is necessary to keep track of all the files created and, if the number of files is known to be small, then the data could be kept in store. The technique of program inversion allows us to combine the two programs into one, thus allowing immediate production of analysis data as soon as all data for a job are assembled.

9.7 Exercises

9.7.1. In respect of the student marks problem (figures 9.12, 9.14 and appendix J), given the following data, show the contents of the entry status indicator, the intermediate file status indicator and the intermediate file record (or equivalent global data areas) for each of the operations affected by the coding rules (that is, 2, 4, 7, 8, 21, 24, 25, 26).

Use a student file of the form:

MATHS	F JONES	35
MATHS	C DODD	48
SCIENCE	J BROWN	62

9.7.2. A stock file contains product detail records comprising: a product group code, a product code, the product description and the stock level. The file is sorted into product code within product group order. An example of the file contents is:

Group	Product code	Description	Stock level
A	1234	NUTS	25
A	1316	BOLTS	13
A	4312	SCREWS	46
C	1625	WOOD GLUE	15
C	2315	SUPER GLUE	29
D	1234	HAMMER	42
D	6678	CHISEL	32

A report is required of all products for which the stock level has fallen below the reserve level of 20. The report is to be paged with standard page headings (title, page number and date). In addition to the product details being printed (one per line), a total of the number of different products selected per product group is to be shown at the end of each group. There is no relationship between product group and page. There could be more than one product group per page, and a product group could span more than one page. You may assume that there are no blank lines in the report.

Design a program to produce this report by following these steps:

(a) Draw logical data structures for the stock file and report, and then, as you attempt to find correspondences, you should identify a boundary clash.

    (b) For program 1 (produce intermediate file from stock file), go through
        each stage from logical data structures to program structure with
        allocated operations and conditions.
    (c) Repeat (b) for program 2 (produce report from intermediate file).
    (d) Indicate how you would amend certain operations and include others
        to make one program a subprogram of the other.

9.7.3. Describe in your own words

    (a) 'Why structure clashes occur'
    (b) 'How program inversion aids the solution of structure clashes'.

    If you wish, you may now attempt the case study in appendix C.

10 Recognition Problems and Backtracking

10.1 Introduction

For most problems we can 'find our way' through the program structure by reading one record ahead. By inspecting the next record to be processed (that is, the record just read), we can determine whether or not there is a further occurrence of the iterated part of an iteration and which part of a selection is to be executed.

Sometimes, however, we need to read more than one record ahead. Consider a file of personnel details where for each person there is either one or two records — a financial record and/or a non-financial record. It is possible to have (for any person) either one of the records, or both records in either order. We have a structure as shown in figure 10.1.

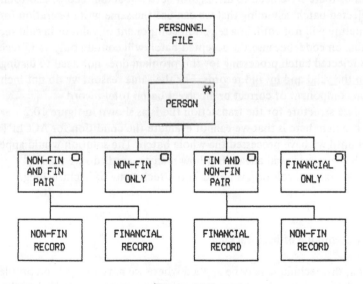

Figure 10.1

The problem with this structure is that we cannot construct the conditions unless we have the next two records to be processed available for selection. So we introduce a two record read ahead.

A simple two record read ahead routine might be:

Copy area-2 into area-1
If not end of file
    read a record into area-2

This routine would be performed for every record required. That is, it would be performed twice at the beginning and when two records have been processed, and once when one record has been processed.

Now consider the problem of validating a transaction file containing batches of records. Each batch contains a number of detail records followed by a batch total record. Each record is of fixed length, containing a batch number, a code, an amount and the type (detail or total). The amount in the total record is the sum of each detail record (but it could be wrong). The code in the total record is always zeros and does not need validating, but the code in the detail records should be within a specific range. The validation rules state that batches without errors are written to an accepted batches file, and batches with errors are written to a rejected batches file. Also, the computed batch total amount for an accepted batch is displayed at the operator's terminal.

In drawing a logical data structure for the transaction file, we must distinguish between an accepted batch and a rejected batch. For an accepted batch we include only components relevant to the processing of an accepted batch; for example, the computed total is displayed only for an accepted batch. For a rejected batch we include only components relevant to the treatment of a batch known to contain errors; thus there is no need to distinguish between detail records and total records for a rejected batch, assuming that we can use the same write operation for both. The structure will not contain a selection component of valid or invalid record depending on code, because the accepted batch will contain only valid records, and the rejected batch processing for this problem does not need to distinguish between the valid and invalid records. For the same reason, we do not include a selection component of correct or incorrect batch total record.

The data structure for the transaction file is as shown in figure 10.2.

The problem here is that we cannot evaluate the condition for ACCEPTED BATCH until we have processed the whole batch. The solution would appear to be a multiple record read ahead. But how many records do we read?

A more practical solution is found in the technique of backtracking.

10.2 The technique of backtracking

In general, this technique may be applied where we have recognition problems. That is, when the natural and correct program structure cannot be directly implemented because of an inability to recognise the controlling condition for one or more constructs. The solution to such problems is first described by means of an allegory.

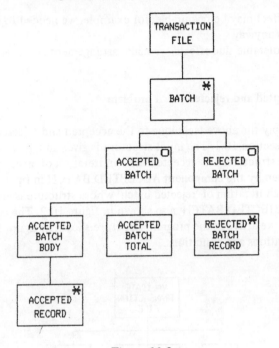

Figure 10.2

Suppose we have two sets of playing cards which are placed face down on a table, and it is known that one set contains an ace (and no kings) and the other set a king (and no aces). How do we select the one with the ace? We cannot know which to select, so we make an arbitrary choice and examine the selected set, a card at a time, until we find the ace (we have made the right choice!) or we find the king (we have made the wrong choice!). In the latter case we now pick up the second set and, if necessary, re-arrange the first set as if it had not been disturbed.

If we cannot make a decision at the outset, then we adopt the following procedure:

1. Make an arbitrary choice (or an informed guess if there are some clues), assuming it to be the correct one. We call this a POSIT.
2. Follow up that choice until such time as it is proved to be right or wrong.
3. If the choice is found to be incorrect, then stop following the choice made (we call this a QUIT) and follow instead the alternative choice (this is called an ADMIT).
4. If by taking the wrong choice we have disturbed something, we must identify the importance of this disturbance. We call such disturbances SIDE EFFECTS.
5. A side effect may be intolerable; for example, we must replace the set of cards in exactly the same place and order.
6. Or a side effect may be neutral (or tolerable); for example, it does not matter that we have disturbed the first set of cards.

7. Or a side effect may be favourable; for example, we needed to move the first
set of cards anyway.
8. For the intolerable side effects, we make arrangements to reverse them.

10.3 The accepted and rejected batch problem

Let us now apply the above technique to the accepted and rejected batch problem
introduced in section 10.1. The input structure is given in figure 10.2.

The output structures are 'accepted file', an iteration of 'accepted batch' whose
structure is given by the component ACCEPTED BATCH in figure 10.2; and
'rejected file', an iteration of 'rejected batch' whose structure is given by the
component REJECTED BATCH, also shown in figure 10.2. The correspondences
being obvious, we arrive at the program structure shown in figure 10.3 with
allocated operations and conditions.

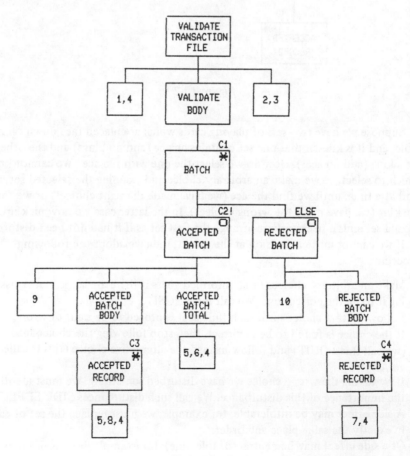

Figure 10.3

The conditions and operations are:

C1 — Until end of file.
C2 — If a valid (accepted) batch!!!
C3 — Until end of batch record (that is, total record).
C4 — Until change of batch or end of file.

1. Open files.
2. Close files.
3. Stop.
4. Read a transaction file record.
5. Write transaction record to accepted file.
6. Display computed batch total.
7. Write transaction record to rejected file.
8. Add amount to batch total.
9. Initialise batch total.
10. Store batch number.

We now continue with the design process and produce schematic logic, omitting the reference to condition C2. This gives the schematic logic shown in figure 10.4.

```
VALIDATE TRANSACTION FILE SEQ
    DO 1  [Open files
    DO 4  [Read a transaction file record
    VALIDATE BODY ITER UNTIL C1 [end of file
      BATCH SEL
        ACCEPTED BATCH SEQ
          DO 9  [Initialise batch total
          ACCEPTED BATCH BODY ITER UNTIL C3 [end of batch record
            ACCEPTED RECORD
              DO 5  [Write transaction record to accepted file
              DO 8  [Add amount to batch total
              DO 4  [Read a transaction file record
            ACCEPTED RECORD END
          ACCEPTED BATCH BODY END
          ACCEPTED BATCH TOTAL
            DO 5  [Write transaction record to accepted file
            DO 6  [Display computed batch total
            DO 4  [Read a transaction file record
          ACCEPTED BATCH TOTAL END
        ACCEPTED BATCH END
      BATCH ELSE 1
        REJECTED BATCH SEQ
          DO 10  [Store batch number
          REJECTED BATCH BODY ITER UNTIL C4 [change of batch or end of file
            REJECTED RECORD
              DO 7  [Write transaction record to rejected file
              DO 4  [Read a transaction file record
            REJECTED RECORD END
          REJECTED BATCH BODY END
        REJECTED BATCH END
      BATCH END
    VALIDATE BODY END
    DO 2  [Close files
    DO 3  [Stop
VALIDATE TRANSACTION FILE END
```

Figure 10.4

Next we amend the schematic logic by adopting the following procedure:

(a) Replace the BATCH SEL by BATCH POSIT.
(b) Replace the BATCH ELSE 1 by BATCH ADMIT.
(c) Identify the points in the accepted batch procedures where it may become known that the batch is invalid and insert QUIT statements.

   Two QUITs from BATCH POSIT are necessary:

(i) If the code in a detail record is invalid (not in range).
(ii) If the computed batch total is not equal to the total in the batch total record.

   We insert the first at the beginning of ACCEPTED RECORD, and the second at the beginning of ACCEPTED BATCH TOTAL. The conditions for the QUITs are added to the condition list:

C5 — If invalid code.
C6 — If computed total not = total in the batch total record.

(Occasionally, though not in this case, it may be necessary to support a condition by including additional operations before a QUIT.)

(d) Identify and classify side effects. We look at all operations in the ACCEPTED BATCH process that come logically before the last QUIT. Hence:

(i) Operation 9 [Initialise batch total] is a neutral side effect.
(ii) Operation 5 [Write transaction record to accepted file], in ACCEPTED RECORD, is an intolerable side effect because, if the batch turns out to be a rejected one, none of its records should be written to the accepted file.
(iii) Operation 8 [Add amount to batch total] is a neutral side effect because, although it is unnecessary to the REJECTED BATCH process, it will not interfere with it, and anyway its effects are cancelled at the beginning of a new batch.
(iv) Operation 4 [Read a transaction file record], after operation 8, is an intolerable side effect because a read statement for a serial or sequential file advances past the last record read, and it is necessary to process the records in a rejected batch from the beginning of the batch.

(e) Insert operations to overcome the intolerable side effects.

   For (ii) above, we need to postpone the output to the accepted file by writing it to a temporary file. This means

11. Initialise temporary file (reset to beginning if necessary)

is allocated right at the beginning of BATCH POSIT.
The first operation 5 becomes

5A. Write transaction record to temporary file.

Then

12. Copy temporary file contents to accepted file

is included immediately after the last QUIT.
(The coding of operation 11 must allow for the situation where the temporary file
has remained open owing to a prior quit from the accepted batch process.)

For (iv) we need to undo the reading of the transaction file by repositioning to
the beginning of the current batch. This means

13. Store position of start of the batch

is allocated at the beginning of BATCH POSIT, and

14. Reposition the transaction file to start of the current batch

is allocated right at the beginning of BATCH ADMIT.
The modified schematic logic is given in figure 10.5.

```
VALIDATE TRANSACTION FILE SEQ
  DO 1  [Open files
  DO 4  [Read a transaction file record
  VALIDATE BODY ITER UNTIL C1 [end of file
    BATCH POSIT (Batch is an accepted batch)
      DO 11  [Initialise temporary file
      DO 13  [Store position of start of the batch
      ACCEPTED BATCH SEQ
        DO 9  [Initialise batch total
        ACCEPTED BATCH BODY ITER UNTIL C3 [end of batch record
          ACCEPTED RECORD
            QUIT BATCH POSIT IF C5 [invalid code
            DO 5A [Write transaction record to temporary file
            DO 8  [Add amount to batch total
            DO 4  [Read a transaction file record
          ACCEPTED RECORD END
        ACCEPTED BATCH BODY END
        ACCEPTED BATCH TOTAL.
          QUIT BATCH POSIT IF C6 [computed total not = total in the
                                 batch total record
          DO 12 [Copy temporary file contents to accepted file
          DO 5  [Write transaction record to accepted file
          DO 6  [Display computed batch total
          DO 4  [Read a transaction file record
        ACCEPTED BATCH TOTAL END
      ACCEPTED BATCH END
    BATCH ADMIT (Batch is not accepted)
      DO 14  [Reposition the transaction file to the start of
              the current batch
      REJECTED BATCH SEQ
        DO 10  [Store batch number
        REJECTED BATCH BODY ITER UNTIL C4 [change of batch or end of file
          REJECTED RECORD
            DO 7  [Write transaction record to rejected file
            DO 4  [Read a transaction file record
          REJECTED RECORD END
        REJECTED BATCH BODY END
      REJECTED BATCH END
    BATCH END
  VALIDATE BODY END
  DO 2  [Close files
  DO 3  [Stop
VALIDATE TRANSACTION FILE END
```

Figure 10.5

10.4 Implementing QUITs

We shall now consider another typical validation situation, which would normally be part of a larger problem, and then illustrate the coding required for QUITs.

A record has three fields: a code, a type and a part number. The record is valid if, and only if, all three fields are valid. The structure of the record can be shown simply as in figure 10.6.

This structure shows clearly that we are interested in only two possibilities. The record is either valid or it is invalid. If it is invalid, we wish to regard it merely as a bad or rejected record. If it is valid we wish to process the fields code, type and part number in certain specific ways. What the structure does not show is that we cannot evaluate the selection between valid record and invalid record so simply. This is because the processing of the first field (code) establishes the conditions for validating the second field (type), and the processing of the second field establishes the conditions for validating the third field (part number). So we begin the processing of the record as if it were a valid record, and take steps to recognise at a later stage that what we may have is an invalid record.

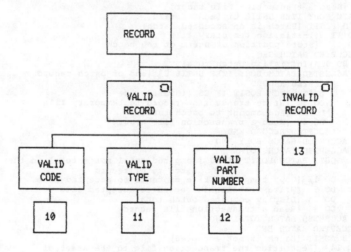

Figure 10.6

Employing the POSIT/ADMIT construct we have the schematic logic as shown in figure 10.7 (note that elementary components have been omitted for clarity).

The COBOL coding for this example is given in figure 10.8.

In PASCAL, we might code the example as shown in figure 10.9.

Finally, the outline coding for BASIC is given in figure 10.10.

Note the strictly controlled use of GOTO. For each QUIT we go to the ADMIT branch. At the end of the POSIT branch, we go to the end of the POSIT/ADMIT component.

```
RECORD POSIT (a valid record)
  VALID RECORD SEQ
    QUIT RECORD POSIT IF C1   [code is invalid
    DO 10   [Process code
    QUIT RECORD POSIT IF C2   [type is invalid
    DO 11   [Process type
    QUIT RECORD POSIT IF C3   [part number is invalid
    DO 12   [Process part number
  VALID RECORD END
RECORD ADMIT  (an invalid record)
  DO 13   [Process error record
RECORD END
```

Figure 10.7

```
    RECORD-POSIT.
    VALID-RECORD-SEQ.
        IF CODE-ERROR GO TO RECORD-ADMIT.
        Process code
        IF TYPE-ERROR GO TO RECORD-ADMIT.
        Process type
        IF PART-NO-ERROR GO TO RECORD-ADMIT.
        Process part number
    VALID-RECORD-END.
        GO TO RECORD-END.
    RECORD-ADMIT.
        Process error record
    RECORD-END.
```

Figure 10.8

```
    LABEL 30,40;

        (* record posit - a valid record *)
          (* valid record seq *)
            IF CODEERROR THEN GOTO 30;
            Process code
            IF TYPEERROR THEN GOTO 30;
            Process type
            IF PARTNOERROR THEN GOTO 30;
            Process part number
          (* valid record end *)
            GOTO 40;
    30: (* record admit - an invalid record *)
            Process error record
    40: (* record end *)
```

Figure 10.9

```
100   REM ** record posit - a valid record **
110     REM ** valid record seq **
120        IF (code is in error) GOTO 200
130        Process code
140        IF (type is in error) GOTO 200
150        Process type
160        IF (part number is in error) GOTO 200
170        Process part number
180     REM ** valid record end **
190     GOTO 220
200   REM ** record admit - an invalid record **
210     Process error record
220   REM ** record end **
```

Figure 10.10

10.5 Dealing with intolerable side effects

Having classified the side effects as favourable, neutral or intolerable by examining each operation of the POSIT that comes logically before the last QUIT, we must overcome the intolerable side effects. We shall now summarise the main techniques.

Consider the situation where POSIT processing may change the state of certain variables, but ADMIT needs the original states. This can be catered for by storing (or freezing) the state of computation on entry to the POSIT, and restoring (or unfreezing) on entry to the ADMIT. For example, on entry to POSIT we may store a copy of the contents of all variables whose state is (or may be) changed by POSIT processing; then if the ADMIT component is entered, the values would be restored from the temporary copy area.

Serial access read operations in the POSIT can give rise to intolerable side effects (for example, 'read a transaction file record' in the problem of section 10.3) as ADMIT may need to access the records read past. This can be overcome, as indicated in section 10.3, by storing the position of the file at the beginning of the POSIT and then repositioning the file to the stored position right at the beginning of the ADMIT.

The basic principle employed in both the above situations is the same – store at the start of POSIT and restore at the start of ADMIT.

Output operations in the POSIT can also lead to intolerable side effects. As we saw in section 10.3, the first occurrence of 'write transaction record to accepted file' was intolerable, because if the batch turns out to be a rejected one, none of its records should be written to the accepted file. We therefore replaced the above write by 'write transaction record to temporary file' and then copied the contents of the temporary file to the accepted file immediately after the last QUIT.

Even if POSIT and ADMIT processing output to the same file, the actual output may differ. In the valid and invalid record problem of section 10.4, the processing of valid code and valid type could be 'print the contents of the field with a suitable comment', with no printing required for a valid part number or an invalid record. In this case, with only two lines to deal with, we would replace each print operation by 'store the print line in a buffer' and then print from the buffers immediately after the last QUIT.

Thus, for output operations, we do not execute the write statement at the point indicated within POSIT, but postpone the output until all QUIT points have been passed.

10.6 QUIT from iteration

If necessary, the QUIT statement can be introduced into the iteration construct. The ordinary form of iteration imposes the constraint that the terminating condition must be capable of evaluation at the head of the loop. In some situations this cannot be satisfied without introducing switches, which inevitably makes the structure more complex. There may be several circumstances under which the iteration is to be terminated, and they may not all be capable of evaluation at the head of the loop. In some processes, such as table searching, some of the processing within the iteration component must be completed before exiting, or some of the processing may be necessary for elaboration of the terminating condition. We therefore introduce the QUIT statement into the iteration construct.

Consider the sequential table search problem where it is required to attempt to match a 'target' with one of the table elements. The table elements are already sorted into ascending order. The table search is over as soon as the target is matched or as soon as a match is not possible (that is, when target is less than the current table element being compared). We assume the last element of the table contains an impossibly high value.

The program structure with allocated operations and conditions would include the components shown in figure 10.11.

The conditions and operations are:

C1 – If target = current element.
C2 – If target < current element.

6. Process matched target.
7. Process unmatched target.
8. Increment index.
9. Initialise index.

The schematic logic with appropriate quit points is shown in figure 10.12.

You will notice that, in this case, both QUITs are unconditional. However, as you will see from the first exercise, a QUIT from iteration can have an associated condition.

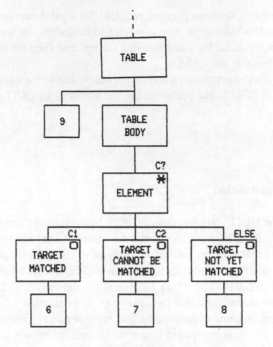

Figure 10.11

```
TABLE SEQ
   DO 9    [Initialise index
   TABLE BODY ITER (? condition)
      ELEMENT SEL IF Cl [target = current element
         TARGET MATCHED
            DO 6    [Process matched target
            QUIT TABLE BODY ITER
         TARGET MATCHED END
      ELEMENT ELSE 1 IF C2 [target < current element
         TARGET CANNOT BE MATCHED
            DO 7    [Process unmatched target
            QUIT TABLE BODY ITER
         TARGET CANNOT BE MATCHED END
      ELEMENT ELSE 2
         TARGET NOT YET MATCHED
            DO 8    [Increment index
         TARGET NOT YET MATCHED END
      ELEMENT END
   TABLE BODY END
TABLE END
```

Figure 10.12

If you wish, you may attempt the case study in appendix D after completing
the following exercises.

10.7 Exercises

10.7.1. Amend the schematic logic of the table search example given above to:

    (a) Store an element description if the element is found (that is, as in a code translation).

    (b) Allow for there not being a last element with an impossibly high value (that is, it is necessary to test the index against a maximum).

10.7.2. A chain store file contains records, each containing a department code, record type indicator and other fields. A type 1 record contains the start-of-day cash figure; a type 2 record the end-of-day cash figure. A program is required that will detect errors and store correct data in an accepted file. If the data for a department are valid, they are written to the accepted file; if invalid in any way, the data are rejected and the following message displayed:

INCORRECT DATA FOR DEPARTMENT nnnnnn

    Data for a department are valid if:

    (i) There are exactly 2 records for the department, a type 1 and a type 2 record, in that order.

    (ii) The value of both cash fields is in the range £100 to £100,000.

    (iii) The value of cash at the end of day on the type 2 record is strictly greater than the value of cash at the start of the day on the type 1 record.

    The records are sorted into ascending order of record type indicator within department code.

    Design the program to detect the above errors and produce appropriate output by following these steps:

    (a) Construct logical data structures for

        • the chain store file
        • the accepted file.

    (b) Identify correspondences and produce a program structure.

    (c) List the elementary operations and conditions.

    (d) Allocate these to the program structure.

    (e) Revise the program structure to include body boxes, if necessary.

    (f) Produce schematic logic.

    (g) Revise the schematic logic to introduce as appropriate POSIT, ADMIT and QUIT.

    (h) Classify any side effects.

    (i) Amend the operation list and condition list to cater for side effect processing and QUITs.

    (j) Revise the schematic logic to incorporate side effect processing.

11 Procedurisation

11.1 Introduction

We shall use the term 'procedure' in a general sense to include those parts of a complete program variously called subprograms, functions, subroutines and segments. In general, procedurisation is used to break the problem down into more manageable parts to facilitate detail design, testing and maintenance. However the programmer is often faced with the dilemma of deciding which parts to procedurise. In addition to run-time overheads and the problems of interfacing, the ill-advised use of procedures can lead to implementation and maintenance problems rather than to their reduction. The programmer should therefore always have sound reasons for procedurising and, in doing so, should ensure that the principles of JSP are not contradicted. For example, in chapter 9 we used a subprogram, with good reason, to solve the structure clash problem by considering two simpler problems instead. The purpose of this chapter is to provide some general guidelines on procedurisation within the context of JSP.

11.2 Bottom-up procedures

A programmer should be aware of and make use of, with due consideration for portability, the available facilities (such as string handling routines, sort routines etc.), whether these are provided by the programming language or a library. However, if the base design level, as defined by the facilities of the target language and the available library routines, does not contain the required operations or data structures, then such facilities can be created. Procedures created in this way are often termed 'bottom-up' procedures. The decision to use them could be made on inspection of the problem specification (that is, before data structures are produced).

For example, suppose it is required to produce a piece of software based on the processing of days of the week. Irrespective of the overall task to be accomplished, it could be decided that the following basic facilities are needed:

(a) A data structure to represent days of the week.
(b) Routines for the input, output and comparison of the days of the week.

Given that these facilities are not present in the target language, they would have to be constructed. Thus, the base level is raised in the sense that 'write day of the week', for example, could then be regarded as an elementary operation and coded by a procedure call.

11.3 Top-down procedures

Consider the fragment shown in figure 11.1 from a program structure.

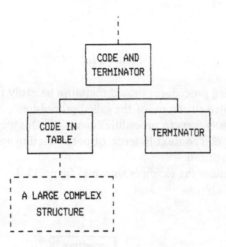

Figure 11.1

If we assume that CODE IN TABLE is large or complex, then the program quality may be improved by making CODE IN TABLE a separate procedure. Such a decision could be made when developing the program structure, before operations and conditions are allocated.

This would mean:

1. Separating the structures, so that in effect CODE IN TABLE becomes an elementary component of the higher level structure, as shown in figure 11.2. Note that the references 3.4/CODE-SUB and 3.4/MAINPROG are used to link the two structures for documentation purposes.
2. When allocating operations

    12. Derive table code (say)

    would be allocated to CODE IN TABLE.
3. At the coding stage this operation would then be coded by the procedure call.

Similarly, if the structure subordinate to TERMINATOR is large or complex, then this could also be procedurised. The purpose of such procedurisation is primarily to enhance readability. The overall process performed by the higher level

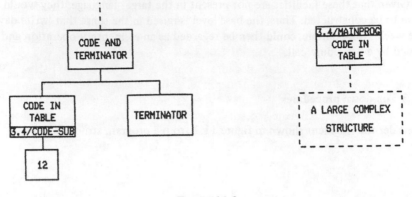

Figure 11.2

structure (the calling procedure) should therefore be easily perceived without recourse to the detailed structures of the called procedures.

There are no parameters to procedures created in this way because they are dependent on program context in terms of both function and interface. Parameters would be artificial.

Let us now consider the example shown in figure 11.3.

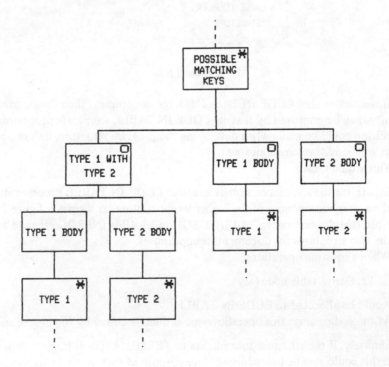

Figure 11.3

We shall assume that the structures with allocated operations and conditions subordinate to both occurrences of TYPE 1 BODY are non-trivial and identical. We can then avoid repetition of the same code, and hence reduce program size, by using a procedure for TYPE 1 BODY. This is known as coding optimisation. Obviously, the decision to use procedures in this way can be taken only by inspecting the program structure with allocated operations and conditions. The procedure is implemented using the steps outlined in the previous example. Once again we have the advantage of enhanced readability. Similarly, if the structures with allocated operations and conditions subordinate to the components TYPE 2 BODY were identical, then they could also be procedurised.

However, in making the decision to optimise on space, we must be aware of the consequences. Using the same procedure in two different contexts means that it may have to be parameterised. The program may also be more difficult to debug and modify. If an error occurs in such a procedure, unless we had detailed tracing information, we would not know from which part of the program it had been called. A minor modification to the program specification could mean that the structures subordinate to the components TYPE 1 BODY were no longer identical, in which case the procedure could no longer be used. For this reason, if the decision to optimise is taken, one should always preserve the unoptimised design.

Let us now assume that the structure with allocated operations and conditions for TYPE 1 BODY is similar, but not identical, to that for TYPE 2 BODY. Some programmers may then be tempted to devise a general procedure which could be used for both TYPE 1 BODY and TYPE 2 BODY. This form of procedurisation is not recommended. The program code should always be derived from the program structure which, in turn, must be derived from the data structures. The program structure should never be modified merely to allow procedurisation to be used.

Finally, a word of warning. Problems can arise if procedures are used within programs involving inversion or backtracking. Both these techniques require the use of GOTO, but transferring control from one procedure to another invariably causes problems. The precise effect of such a jump can vary from one language to another; it may even vary between implementations of a particular language, and it may even depend on the type of procedure being used (for example, PERFORM or CALL in COBOL). It is not the intention therefore to discuss this problem in any depth, but merely to remind you that:

1. To maintain continuity within an inverted program, a statement is inserted at the beginning of the subprogram to transfer control to the point in the code from which we last exited (see chapter 9). If the subprogram is itself procedurised, then this could mean jumping out of one procedure to the middle of another.
2. The QUIT in backtracking involves jumping from the POSIT to the ADMIT structure. If they are in separate procedures, then once again the results could be unpredictable.

12 Interactive Systems

12.1 Interactive dialogue

Many systems allow individual users to interact with the computer directly. This involves the use of a dialogue between a terminal user and the computer. The most common basic types of interactive dialogue are:

(a) menu selection
(b) form filling
(c) question and answer
(d) interrogate or command.

In this chapter we develop program structures with allocated operations and conditions for each of the above. Each example is considered to be part of a larger problem – in practice it could be a self-contained procedure – and therefore we include only the structure, operations and conditions relevant to the dialogue.

When considering data structures for a screen dialogue it could be argued that, as far as the program is concerned, the screen includes both input data, because user responses are 'accepted', and output data, because text is 'displayed'. However, all data on the screen, whether regarded as input or output, must appear sequentially, for example, prompt (output) then user response (input) and so on. Thus, there is no point in producing two separate structures, and we shall develop just one data structure for each screen.

12.2 Menu selection

Consider the menu selection dialogue shown in figure 12.1.

The whole menu is used repeatedly until a user response of 'E' is received. If the user types anything other than A, D, I, R or E, an error message inviting him to try again is displayed at the bottom of the screen; the message is erased once the user has tried again. Valid responses invoke calls to separate procedures (one per option). A possible procedure for the ADD option is developed in the next section.

A logical data structure for this screen consists of an iteration of menu displays,

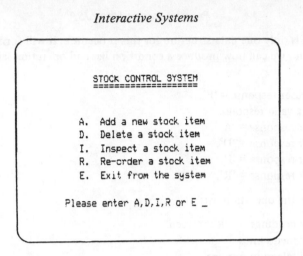

Figure 12.1

each of which is a sequence of the headings, followed by the menu, followed by the prompt, followed by the user response. Since the user must eventually type a valid response after having typed any number of invalid responses (including zero), we show an iteration of invalid responses, followed by a valid response which is either A, D, I, R or E — see figure 12.2.

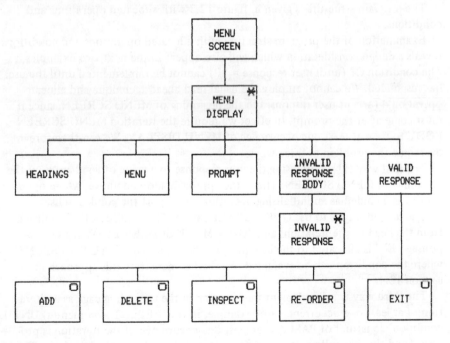

Figure 12.2

As there is only one data structure for this procedure, it will form the program structure, and we can now produce a condition list and operation list. First the condition list:

C1 — Until user response = 'E'.
C2 — Until a valid response.
C3 — If user response = 'A'.
C4 — If user response = 'D'.
C5 — If user response = 'I'.
C6 — If user response = 'R'.

And now the operation list:

1. Display headings on clear screen.
2. Display menu lines.
3. Display selection prompt.
4. Accept user response.
5. Display error message line (try again).
6. Clear error message line.
7. Call 'Add' procedure.
8. Call 'Delete' procedure.
9. Call 'Inspect' procedure.
10. Call 'Re-order' procedure.
11. Initialise user response (to space).

The program structure is given in figure 12.3 with allocated operations and conditions.

Examination of the program structure with allocated operations and conditions reveals a design consideration which will also appear in the next two examples. The condition C1 (until user response = 'E') cannot be implemented until the user has responded. We cannot employ the usual read ahead technique and allocate operation 4 (accept user response) to the beginning of MENU SCREEN, since it must come after the prompt. In effect we require the iteration MENU SCREEN BODY to have at least one occurrence of MENU DISPLAY. We can therefore overcome the problem in three ways.

The first way is by initialising the user response to a value other than 'E' at the beginning of MENU SCREEN. This is the approach adopted above, where operation 11 is included as an initialising operation to support the condition list.

The second way is to use QUIT out of iteration. The condition C1 is omitted from the head of the iteration, and "QUIT MENU SCREEN BODY if user response = 'E' " is allocated to the beginning of the component VALID RESPONSE where the condition can be evaluated. We shall demonstrate this approach in section 12.4.

The third way is to implement the iteration in the target language as an iteration of at least one occurrence. For example, in the 'REPEAT statement(s) UNTIL condition' construct of PASCAL, at least one occurrence of the iteration is processed and the controlling condition is evaluated at the bottom of the loop. This

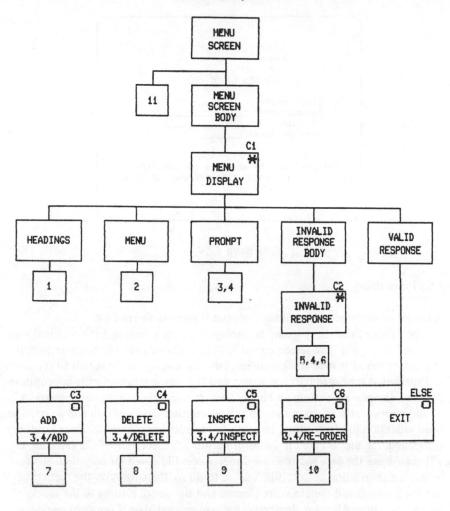

Figure 12.3

can be implemented in COBOL and BASIC by removing the code for 'if condition go to end of the iteration' from the start of the iteration and, at the end of the iteration, replacing the code for 'go to start of iteration' by the code for 'if not condition go to the start of the iteration'.

Having overcome the above problem, note that we can use a read ahead technique for the iteration INVALID RESPONSE BODY. We allocate operation 4 as soon as the prompt has been displayed, and once for every time the user must repeat to correct an error.

```
STOCK CONTROL SYSTEM
====================

      ADD NEW STOCK ITEM

Stock number    _____
Description     _____
Location        _____
Re-order level  ____.__


Confirm that the above is correct (Y/N)  _
Do you wish to repeat this transaction (Y/N)  _
```

Figure 12.4

12.3 Form filling

A simple example of a form filling dialogue is given in figure 12.4.

The whole of the above 'form' is displayed on the screen and the terminal user is guided through it. The screen cursor is first positioned after 'stock number'; if the user enters an invalid stock number, an error message inviting him to try again is displayed at the bottom of the screen and the cursor returns to the appropriate position; the new stock number having been entered, the message disappears. After a valid response, the cursor moves to the description field position and so on. There is no validation for description, location or re-order level. After the four fields are completed, the user is asked if the information is correct; only if the response is affirmative are the data written to a direct access file. The user may then elect to repeat the transaction or not; if he wishes to do so, the entries on the form (but not the headings and skeleton) are cleared and the cursor returns to the stock number position. Also, for simplicity, we assume that Y or N (yes/no) responses are not validated (Y means yes, anything else means no).

The logical data structure is more complicated than for the menu selection — see figure 12.5. Note that stock number is shown as a sequence of an iteration of invalid entries (possibly zero) followed by a valid entry. This is because the user is forced to enter a valid stock number before continuing, after (possibly) entering a number of invalid ones.

Assuming that the record is written to a direct access file, we have no other data structures to take into account, the data structure then becomes the program structure and we can list the conditions and operations.

The condition list is:

C1 — Until user no longer wants to add new stock items
        (that is, until repeat response $<>$ 'Y').
C2 — Until stock number is a valid one.

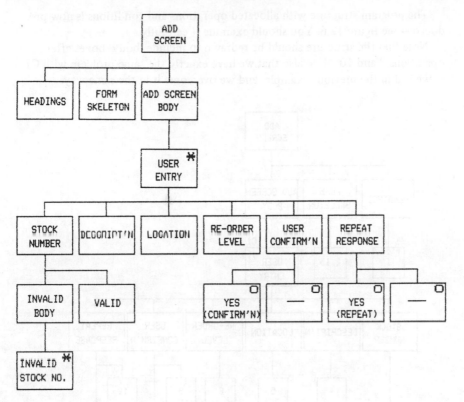

Figure 12.5

C3 If user confirmation – 'Y'.
C4 – If repeat response = 'Y'.

The operation list is:

1. Display headings on clear screen.
2. Display form skeleton (that is, as in figure 12.4).
3. Accept stock number.
4. Accept description.
5. Accept location.
6. Accept re-order level.
7. Display error message line.
8. Clear error message line.
9. Accept confirm response.
10. Accept repeat response.
11. Clear form entries.
12. Write new stock item record.
13. Initialise repeat response (= 'Y').

The program structure with allocated operations and conditions is now produced — see figure 12.6. You should examine it carefully.

Note that the structure should be redrawn to include 'body' boxes after
operations 9 and 10. Note also that we have exactly the same problem with C1
as we had in the previous example, and we overcome it in the same way.

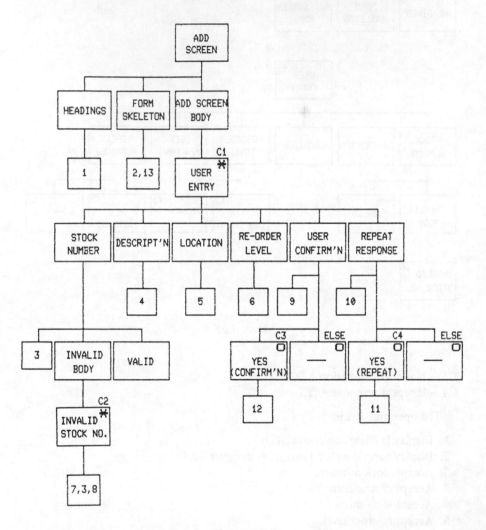

Figure 12.6

12.4 Question and answer

This type of dialogue, although normally not difficult to analyse, may often appear
tedious when drawing data structures. We will consider a simple one by examining

an example conversation which could be used to view the data of the previous example. The user input is underlined.

```
WHAT STOCK NUMBER? 10004
ACCESS NOT ALLOWED
DO YOU WISH TO TRY AGAIN? Y
WHAT STOCK NUMBER? 95006
DOES NOT EXIST
DO YOU WISH TO TRY AGAIN? Y
WHAT STOCK NUMBER? 25632
O.K. WHAT FIELD? RE-ORD LEVEL
DOES NOT EXIST
DO YOU WISH TO TRY AGAIN? Y
WHAT STOCK NUMBER? 2563
O.K. WHAT FIELD? LOCATION
ACCESS NOT ALLOWED
DO YOU WISH TO TRY AGAIN? Y
WHAT STOCK NUMBER? 26321
O.K. WHAT FIELD? DESCRIPTION
O.K. BROWN LEATHER BOOTS SIZE 6
DO YOU WISH TO TRY AGAIN? N
EXIT
```

We can see that there are only three basic questions which lead to a number of responses by the user. The user's response determines what happens next. The response to 'WHAT STOCK NUMBER?' may be valid, with or without access rights, or invalid. If the number is valid (that is, if it exists) and the user has access rights, then he is asked to specify which field he wishes to view (O.K. WHAT FIELD?). Possible responses to this question are valid field names, with or without access rights, or an invalid field name. Entering a valid field name with access rights produces the appropriate data value (O.K. BROWN LEATHER BOOTS SIZE 6). Whenever an invalid stock number or invalid field is entered, the same message (DOES NOT EXIST) is displayed; similarly, whenever access is not allowed, the same message (ACCESS NOT ALLOWED) is displayed. Once either of these messages or the appropriate data has been displayed, the user is invited to re-try (DO YOU WISH TO TRY AGAIN?). A response of 'Y' leads to a repeat of the above, beginning with 'WHAT STOCK NUMBER?', otherwise the dialogue terminates with EXIT.

We can use the sample dialogue to identify the order and grouping of the data, before drawing the data structure. At the top level we recognise that the dialogue is an iteration of USER REQUEST, which consists of the lines from 'WHAT STOCK NUMBER?' to 'DO YOU WISH TO TRY AGAIN?'. This, in turn, is a sequence of STOCK NUMBER, consisting of the lines prior to 'DO YOU WISH TO TRY AGAIN?', followed by the try again question. Then, by incorporating the appropriate selections, we arrive at the data structure shown in figure 12.7.

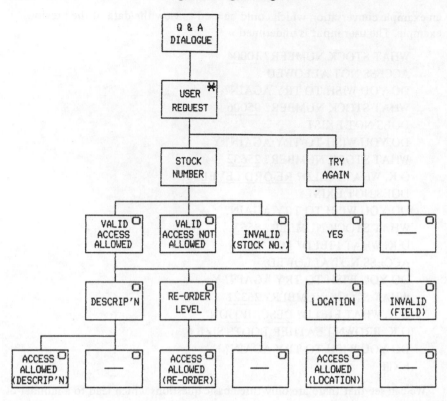

Figure 12.7

This type of deeply nested selection dominated structure can often be simplified by employing the POSIT/ADMIT construct. We could, for each stock number,
presume (or POSIT) a valid request with access rights, resulting in the appropriate
data being displayed, unless forced to admit this is not true. When the admit path
(that is, not valid or no access rights) is taken, we have a simple choice of two
different error messages.

The simplified structure is shown in figure 12.8.

If we assume direct access to the required information, then figure 12.8 is the
only logical data structure that will influence our design. We can, therefore, proceed with the condition list and operation list.

C1 – Until user requests no more
     (that is, until user response (try again) < > 'Y').
C2 – If field = DESCRIPTION.
C3 – If field = RE-ORDER LEVEL.
C4 – If stock number or field invalid.

1. Display 'what stock number' prompt.
2. Accept user response (stock number).

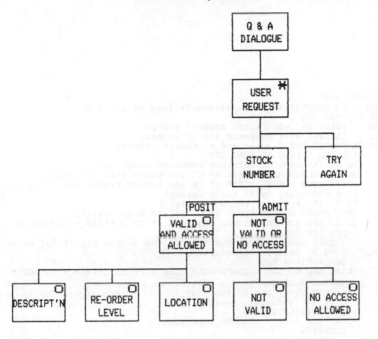

Figure 12.8

3. Display 'try again' prompt.
4. Accept user response (try again).
5. Display 'does not exist'.
6. Display 'what field' prompt.
7. Accept user response (field).
8. Attempt to retrieve required stock item.
9. Display description.
10. Display re-order level.
11. Display location.
12. Display 'exit'.
13. Display 'access not allowed'.

Once again the condition C1 is difficult to implement until the user has had an opportunity to respond to the 'try again' question. It should be noted that, by including the question right at the beginning of the dialogue as well, we would remove the difficulty, as we could then use the standard read ahead technique. Nevertheless, in this example, we demonstrate how QUIT from iteration can overcome the problem. The allocation of the conditions and operations to the program structure is fairly easy, so for demonstration purposes only, we will go straight to the schematic logic — see figure 12.9. You should examine it carefully, paying particular attention to the QUITs from POSIT and the QUIT from iteration.

```
Q+A DIALOGUE SEQ
   Q+A DIALOGUE BODY ITER (no condition defined at the top)
      USER REQUEST SEQ
         DO 1  [Display 'what stock number' prompt
         DO 2  [Accept user response (stock number)
         STOCK NUMBER POSIT valid and allowable request
            VALID AND ACCESS ALLOWED SEQ
               DO 8   [Attempt to retrieve required stock item
               QUIT STOCK NUMBER POSIT IF C5 [no stock item retrieved
               QUIT STOCK NUMBER POSIT IF C6 [no access rights for stock item
               DO 6  [Display 'what field' prompt
               DO 7  [Accept user response (field)
               QUIT STOCK NUMBER POSIT IF C7 [field name invalid
               VALID AND ACCESS ALLOWED BODY SEL IF C2 [ field = DESCRIPTION
                  DESCRIPTION
                     QUIT STOCK NUMBER POSIT IF C8 [no access rights for description
                     DO 9  [Display description
                  DESCRIPTION END
               VALID AND ACCESS ALLOWED BODY ELSE 1 IF C3 [field = RE-ORDER LEVEL
                  RE-ORDER LEVEL
                     QUIT STOCK NUMBER POSIT IF C9 [no access rights for re-order level
                     DO 10  [Display re-order level
                  RE-ORDER LEVEL END
               VALID AND ACCESS ALLOWED BODY ELSE 2
                  LOCATION
                     QUIT STOCK NUMBER POSIT IF C10 [no access rights for location
                     DO 11  [Display location
                  LOCATION END
               VALID AND ACCESS ALLOWED BODY END
            VALID AND ACCESS ALLOWED END
         STOCK NUMBER ADMIT request is not (valid and allowable)
            NOT VALID OR NO ACCESS SEL IF C4 [Stock number or field invalid
               NOT VALID
                  DO 5  [Display 'does not exist'
               NOT VALID END
            NOT VALID OR NO ACCESS ELSE 1
               NO ACCESS ALLOWED
                  DO 13 [Display 'access not allowed'
               NO ACCESS ALLOWED END
            NOT VALID OR NO ACCESS END
         STOCK NUMBER END
         TRY AGAIN
            DO 3  [Display try again prompt
            DO 4  [Accept user response (try again)
            QUIT Q+A DIALOGUE BODY ITER IF C1 [try again response <> 'Y'
         TRY AGAIN END
      USER REQUEST END
   Q+A DIALOGUE BODY END
   DO 12 [Display 'exit'
Q+A DIALOGUE END
```

Figure 12.9

12.5 Interrogate or command

Consider a direct access file containing student names, project titles and grade awarded. A simple command language to interrogate this file might consist of three commands: FIND, PRINT and EXIT. The formats could be:

(a) FIND attribute (NAME or TITLE) value (for example, SMITH).
(b) PRINT attribute (NAME, TITLE or GRADE).
(c) EXIT.

An example of the dialogue with computer responses shown in lower case is:

```
FIND NAME SMITH
not found
FIND NAME BROWN
found
PRINT GRADE
c
FIND TOTLE RELATIONAL DATABASE
no such attribute
FIND TITLE RELATIONAL DATABASE
found
PRING NAME
no such command
PRINT NAME
c. j. holmes
EXIT
```

A data structure to reflect this dialogue is quite simple. We obviously have an iteration of command until the user types 'EXIT'. There are three valid commands, so we need to indicate the choice. Then for FIND and PRINT there is a choice of attributes. An attribute value (in the FIND command) may be found or not found. The data structure, which is essentially driven by the possible user inputs, is shown in figure 12.10.

The direct access file has no extra influence on our design; figure 12.10 becomes the program structure.

The conditions are:

C1 – Until user command EXIT.
C2 – If command = FIND.
C3 – If command = PRINT.
C4 – If attribute = NAME.
C5 – If attribute = TITLE.
C6 – If attribute = GRADE.
C7 – If required name found.
C8 – If required title found.

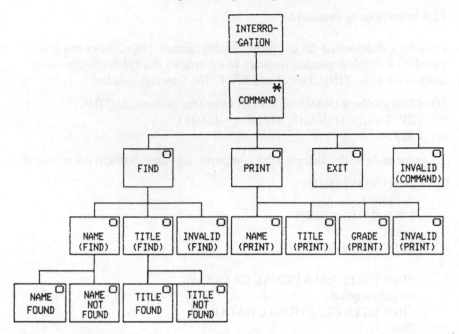

Figure 12.10

The operation list is:

1. Accept command string.
2. Get symbol (command).
3. Get symbol (attribute).
4. Get symbol (value).
5. Attempt to retrieve record with required name.
6. Attempt to retrieve record with required title.
7. Display name.
8. Display title.
9. Display grade.
10. Display 'not found'.
11. Display 'found'.
12. Display 'no such command'.
13. Display 'no such attribute'.
14. Initialise name, title and grade to null.

Note that operations 2 to 4 may well be implemented as a single parameterised subprogram which delivers the required character string. Operation 14 is used so that there is no need to insist on a valid FIND before a PRINT.

The revised program structure with allocated operations and conditions is given in figure 12.11.

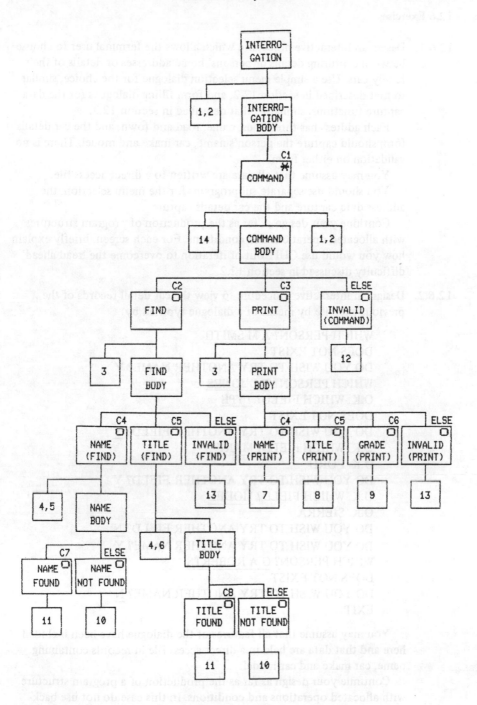

Figure 12.11

12.6 Exercises

12.6.1. Design an interactive procedure which allows the terminal user to choose between capturing details of persons' home addresses or details of their family cars. Use a simple menu selection dialogue for the choice, similar to that described in section 12.2, and form filling dialogues for the data capture functions, similar to that described in section 12.3.

Each address has three lines, name, road and town, and the car details form should capture the person's name, car make and model. There is no validation on either form.

You may assume that all data are written to a direct access file.

You should use separate subprograms for the menu selection, the address data capture and the car details capture.

Continue your design as far as the production of program structures with allocated operations and conditions. For each screen, briefly explain how you would use QUIT out of iteration to overcome the 'read ahead' difficulty discussed in section 12.2.

12.6.2. Design an interactive procedure to view the car detail records of the previous exercise by means of a dialogue typified by:

```
WHICH PERSON? A M SMITH
DOES NOT EXIST
DO YOU WISH TO TRY ANOTHER NAME? Y
WHICH PERSON? F G JONES
O.K. WHICH FIELD? TYPE
DOES NOT EXIST
DO YOU WISH TO TRY ANOTHER FIELD? Y
O.K. WHICH FIELD? MAKE
O.K. FORD
DO YOU WISH TO TRY ANOTHER FIELD? Y
O.K. WHICH FIELD? MODEL
O.K. SIERRA
DO YOU WISH TO TRY ANOTHER FIELD? N
DO YOU WISH TO TRY ANOTHER NAME? Y
WHICH PERSON? G A ROBERTS
DOES NOT EXIST
DO YOU WISH TO TRY ANOTHER NAME? N
EXIT
```

You may assume that all features of the dialogue have been included here and that data are held in a direct access file in records containing name, car make and car model.

Continue your design as far as the production of a program structure with allocated operations and conditions. In this case do not use back-tracking or quit out of iteration.

If you wish, you may now attempt the case study in appendix E.

13 Testing, Documentation and Program Amendment

13.1 Testing

13.1.1 What to test

By now you should appreciate that the main feature of JSP is the way in which we proceed from data structures to program code, through well-defined manageable stages (refer to section 1.4). You should also have realised that if we make a mistake, then certain errors may become apparent at an early stage. For example, if data structures without clashes cannot be combined easily, then the structures should be carefully checked to see if they are correct. If you cannot find an obvious position on the program structure for a certain operation, then you should first ascertain whether or not that operation is necessary and then, provided that it is, check the program structure. Having taken due care in applying the principles and rules of JSP, you should always be reasonably confident that the program is correct.

However, mistakes can still occur and obviously further testing should be incorporated, in keeping with the philosophy of 'identifying errors as soon as possible'. We can test the design once the program structure with allocated operations and conditions has been produced and when we have produced the final schematic logic. In each case, we check the structure, overall logic and data values — in particular, the results to be output. Such details as the correct formats for input and correct layout for output are not included in the elementary operations and therefore cannot be checked until later. They have to be checked at a later stage when testing the program code.

In addition, we may need to test for compatibility with associated software, which means ensuring that programs or subprograms interact correctly. We may also need to test for customer (or user) satisfaction (often called acceptance trials).

13.1.2 Testing the design

We shall describe a method of testing the design by means of a so-called desk check (trace table or dry run) using the program structure with allocated conditions and operations. The principles described apply also to testing the design using the schematic logic. For example, consider the sales report program (figure 5.3 in chapter 5).

Given the program structure with allocated operations and conditions, we must first devise some test data, as considered in section 13.1.4. For illustrative purposes we shall use the following:

	AREA	YEAR	PRODUCT	SALES VALUE
1st record	A	84	PENS	300
2nd record	B	84	PENCILS	500
3rd record	B	85	RUBBERS	50
		end of file indicator		

We then record the results that should be achieved, remembering that, at this stage, we cannot check the precise layout:

> Headings for area A
> Sales 100 to 300 line for 300 pens
> Year total (for 84) of 300
> Area total (for A) of 300
> Headings for area B
> Sales over 300 line for 500 pencils
> Year total (for 84) of 500
> Sales under 100 line for 50 rubbers
> Year total (for 85) of 50
> Area total (for B) of 550

Next we head up a sheet of paper with the names of data areas to be used in the program. One way of doing this for the sales report problem is illustrated in figure 13.1. Then we process the test data by hand, doing only what is indicated by the program structure. Changes to data area contents and the values of conditional expressions are noted. For each output operation we check the current value(s) in the table against the results that should be achieved, for example, the first occurrence of operation 5 should output headings for area A. The start of the trace table is shown in figure 13.1.

We will not complete the desk check here, but invite you to do so. As the test data lead us to the operations and conditions (including the ELSE), they should be ticked off on the program structure.

Finally, when we have exhausted the test data, we check that:

1. We have achieved the correct results.

2. We have ticked off every operation and condition on the program structure. If we have not, we need more exhaustive test data and should repeat the process.

Testing the design will ensure that we have the correct structure, and have correctly allocated operations and conditions. Also it may reveal possible coding pitfalls. For instance, suppose that the appropriate area was to be included in the area total line. As we arrive at operation 6 in the dry run, we would read off a correct value of 300 for area total, a value of B for area and A for stored area. We would then note that stored area (and not area from the current record) should be used when coding operation 6.

OPERATIONS/ CONDITIONS	CURRENT SALES RECORD				STORED AREA	STORED YEAR	AREA TOTAL	YEAR TOTAL	OUTPUT (RESULTS)
	AREA	YEAR	PRODUCT	AMOUNT					
1									
4	A	84	PENS	300					
C1 (false)									✓
5									
13							0		
15					A				
C2 (false)								0	
14									
16						84			
C3 (false)									
C4 (false)									
C5 (true)									✓
9									
11							300		
12								300	
4	B	84	PENCILS	500					
C3 (true)									
7									✓
C2 (true)									
6									✓

Figure 13.1

13.1.3 Testing the coding

We must test the program code to ensure that the elementary operations, conditions and control constructs of the program structure and schematic logic are correctly translated into the target language (see chapter 7). This includes checking the precise details of input and output layouts against the problem specification.

The principles that we have seen in testing the design obviously apply to testing the coding. We must obtain suitable test data; we must know what results are correct and we must aim to test as thoroughly as possible.

Testing the coding will obviously involve using the computer and, as such, the programmer might be able to utilise testing software such as trace programs and debugging aids. These vary considerably from computer to computer so we will not attempt a description here. Rather, we will give a list of the objectives to be met in this aspect of program testing.

1. Ensure that each program statement is executed at least once. This is an obvious point, although it is sometimes not achieved, particularly in the handling of rare error conditions.
2. Ensure that each type of input data has been read at least once. In particular, with variable length fields and records, minimum and maximum lengths should have been specified.
3. Ensure that each type of output data has been written at least once. For example, in printed output check detail lines, headings, total lines, footings etc.
4. Ensure that the terminating condition for each iteration is used. Take care to allow for the alternatives in compound conditions.
5. Ensure that each selection condition is used. Do not forget the ELSE.

6. Ensure that each program statement gives the expected result. Beware of data truncation, rounding, accuracy etc.

13.1.4 Producing test data

Although there are some aids to the production of test data, this job is still viewed as a chore by many programmers, with the result that test data choice is often poor. It is not sufficient merely to test according to simple criteria, such as, there are four record types so we need four records in the test data. A knowledge of the internal states of the program, as revealed by the data structures, should be used to direct the testing.

We can use the data structures, together with the problem specification, to guide us in determining the test data to be used. For example, given the data structure of figure 13.2, let us use it to guide the production of test data.

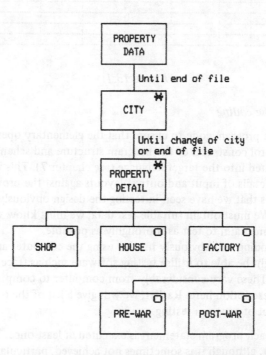

Figure 13.2

(Note that we have included conditions on the diagram for illustrative purposes).

From the first condition we can see that we want at least one CITY and an end of file indication. From the second condition we want to be able to test change of CITY, so we increase our requirement to at least two CITIES. Within the data for a CITY we have data entities for a SHOP, HOUSE, PRE-WAR FACTORY and

POST-WAR FACTORY; so clearly we must have at least one of each of these. There is no relationship between any particular CITY and any property type (any CITY could have any type), so we can conclude that the minimum test data requirement is four property entities (one of each type) with at least one change of CITY.

We have included more than one entity for each iterated part because we have been led to do so by the data structure. It is recommended that there should always be a minimum of two occurrences of an iterated part in order to ensure that the loop is sufficiently tested, especially in respect of the initialisation and incrementation of counters, subscripts and totals.

By examining the problem specification, we might see that the data are to be records containing the fields CITY and PROPERTY TYPE. We could then prepare the data.

record 1	LIVERPOOL	SHOP
record 2	LIVERPOOL	HOUSE
record 3	MANCHESTER	PRE-WAR FACTORY
record 4	MANCHESTER	POST-WAR FACTORY
	end of file indicator	

13.2 Documentation

Documentation should proceed throughout the design process. JSP certainly yields useful documentation at each of the design stages. In this text we have indicated the general way in which structure diagrams and schematic logic could be presented. Specific standards will exist in most computer installations in respect of cross-referencing, size and format. In fact, although attempts are made to provide widely accepted standards of documentation, there is a wide variety of opinion as to what is required and the format of documents.

The principle to guide us is:

The documentation should enable someone other than the originator, but who is familiar with the design methods and documentation standards, to fully understand the program's purpose and the way that purpose has been achieved.

To this end one might consider producing a documentation file for a computer program from the following list:

1. The problem specification including record, screen and print layouts.
2. Data structures.
3. Revised program structure(s) with allocated operations and conditions.
4. Operation and condition lists.
5. Schematic logic(s) (unoptimised).
6. Revised schematic logic(s) when backtracking is used.
7. Optimised schematic logic(s).

8. The source code with suitable comments to describe each component.
9. A test plan with annotated test results.
10. Amendments list.

13.3 Program amendment

It is a fact of life that all applications programs will need amending or enhancing
during their lifetime. Indeed, many programming departments spend a majority
of their resources in program maintenance.

Often programmers do not like the program maintenance task because it may
be tedious and frustrating owing to a lack of adequate documentation or sloppy
programming practice. If a program has been designed according to a reasonable
design method, then the maintenance should be that much easier and satisfying.

From what we have seen of JSP, it should be apparent that amendments
(enhancements) are of two basic types:

(a) functional
(b) structural.

We must first be able to make this distinction. Never be tempted to attempt coding
modifications without first assessing the scale and type of the amendment and
making the changes necessary at each design stage.

A functional amendment is one that merely affects the elementary operations
(or conditions). We might ask ourselves:

'Can I change one (or more) of the existing operations?'
or 'Can I simply add one (or more) operations?'

If we answer 'yes' to either of the above, we can test our answer by (re)allocating
the operation(s) to the program structure. If this task is in any way difficult, then
we should investigate further to see if the amendment is structural.

For a structural amendment, a change is made to one or more of the data
structures. In such a case one proceeds through each stage of the design, making
all necessary changes at each stage.

It is obvious that the distinction between the two types of amendment is crucial
to planning the work of a department. The former will generally take a very short
time, the latter considerably longer.

We defined the main requirements of a software design method (see section 1.2
in chapter 1) as enabling correct programs to be produced and facilitating the
organised control of software projects. Increasingly, most software projects will
involve a high proportion of maintenance as user requirements change. Using JSP
will help the production of correct software and ensure that it remains correct
during its lifetime of inevitable amendment.

13.4 Exercises

13.4.1. Test the design of the program produced for exercise 4.3.2 (see solution for exercise 5.4.2) using the following data:

	WARD	NAME	PATIENT or STAFF
record 1	A100	J G SMITH	PATIENT
record 2	A100	J L THOMAS	PATIENT
record 3	A100	B C WHITE	STAFF
record 4	B300	A B GREEN	STAFF
	end of file indicator		

13.4.2. Test the design of the collate problem from chapter 8 in which only those keys present on one or both of the input files are processed (see figure 8.6 and associated operation and condition lists).
Use the following data:

FILE A (key value)	FILE B (key value)
1235	1468
1468	1532
1532	9999
9999	

(9999 acts as an end of file indicator)

Are the data sufficient?

Appendix A: Solutions to Exercises

The specimen solutions given in this appendix may have equally correct alternatives.

Chapter 2

2.4.1

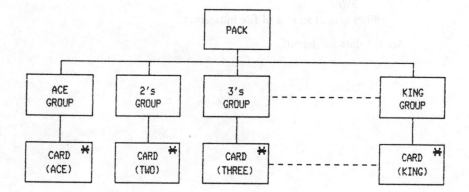

2.4.2

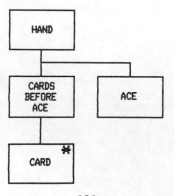

CARDS BEFORE ACE is an iteration of CARD. An iteration may be of zero occurrences, so the minimum number of cards in the hand is one — an ace.

2.4.3

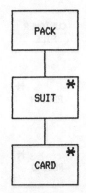

2.4.4

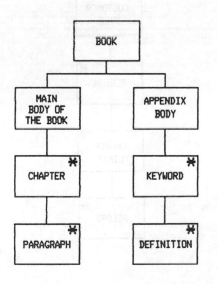

CARDS BEFORE A CHR is an iteration of CARD. An iteration may be of zero occurrences, so the minimum number of cards in the hand is one = zero...

2.4.5

2.4.6

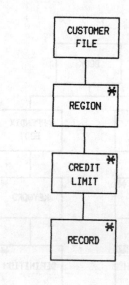

2.4.7

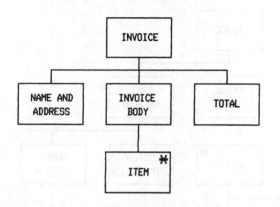

2.4.8

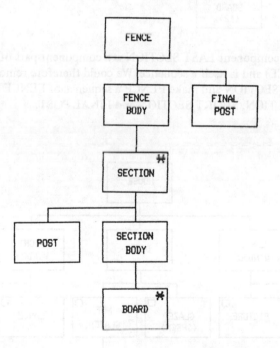

Alternatively, we could regard FENCE as a sequence of FIRST POST followed by
FENCE BODY. SECTION would then be a sequence of SECTION BODY
followed by POST.

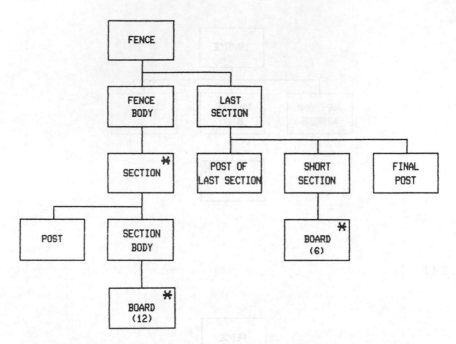

Note that the component LAST SECTION is a component part of a sequence (that is, FENCE) and is itself a sequence. We could therefore remove the component LAST SECTION and make FENCE a sequence of FENCE BODY, POST OF LAST SECTION, SHORT SECTION and FINAL POST.

2.4.10

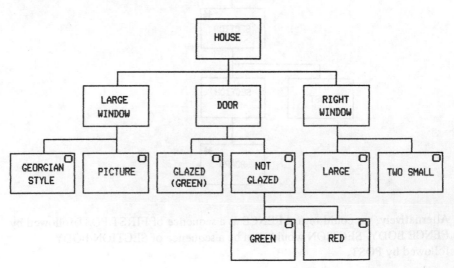

2.4.11

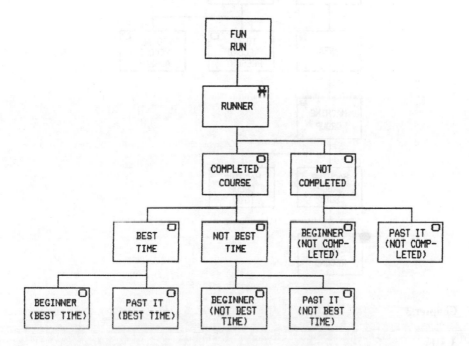

There are a number of possible solutions to this problem because we do not know which of the various selections should be at the top level. More knowledge of the problem we are trying to solve and the physical order of the data would enable us to decide on the most appropriate structure.

2.4.12

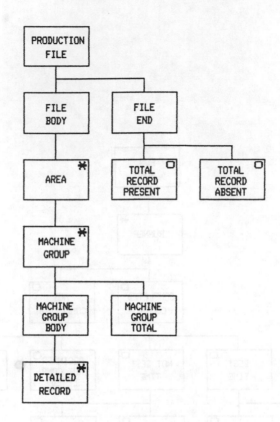

Chapter 3

3.3.1

There are a number of possible solutions to this problem because we do not know whether the second component should be at the top level. More important, some of the procedures we are trying to raise and/or apply would affect the data model above. It is, in fact, better to leave it in the more appropriate situation.

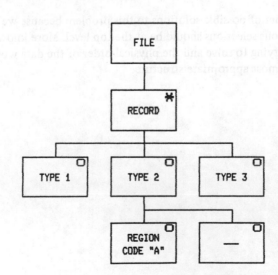

3.3.2   (a)

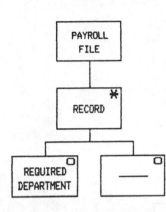

(b)

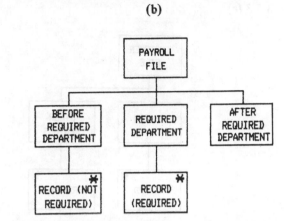

3.3.3   (a)

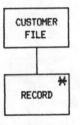

(b)

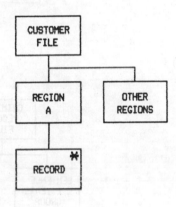

3.3.3   (c)

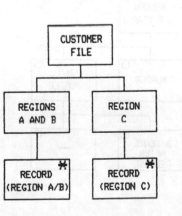

(d)

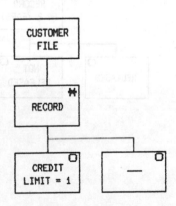

3.3.3 (e)

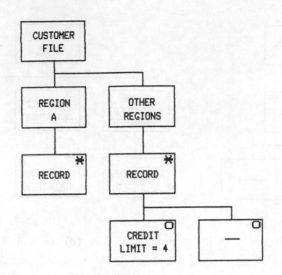

3.3.4 (a)

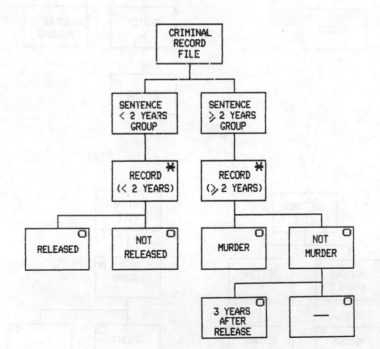

3.3.4 (b)

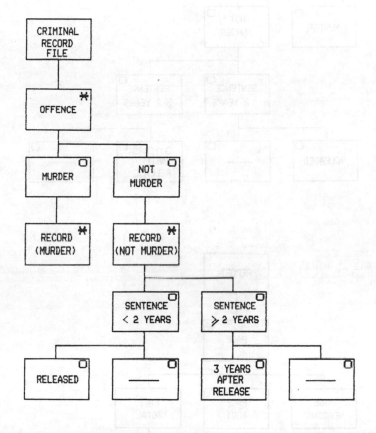

3.3.4 (c)

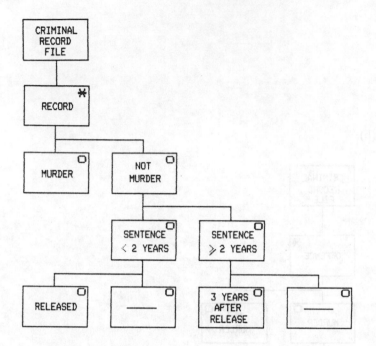

3.3.5

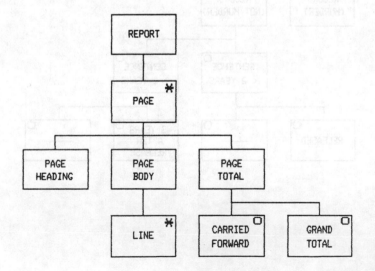

3.3.6

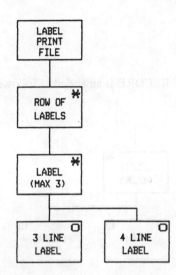

3.3.7 (a)

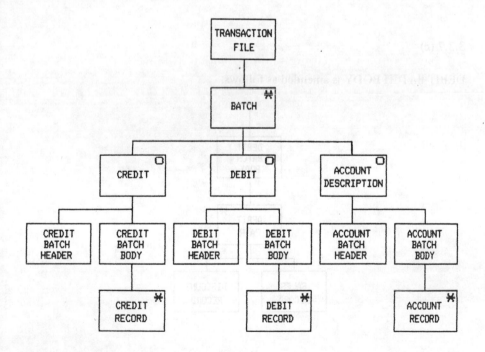

3.3.7 (b)

The component **CREDIT RECORD** is amended as follows:

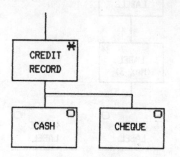

3.3.7 (c)

DEBIT BATCH BODY is amended as follows:

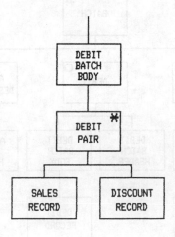

3.3.8 (a)

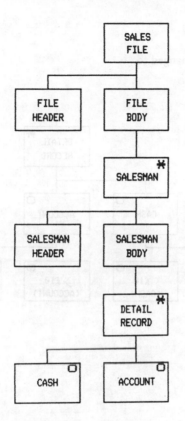

3.3.8 (b)

The component SALESMAN is amended as follows:

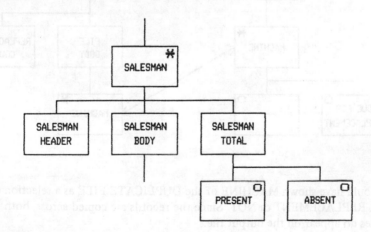

3.3.8 (c)

DETAIL RECORD is changed to:

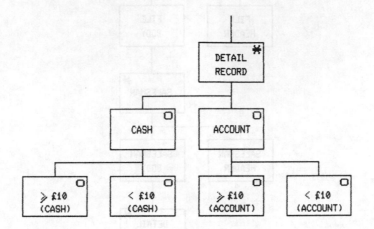

Chapter 4

4.3.1 (a)

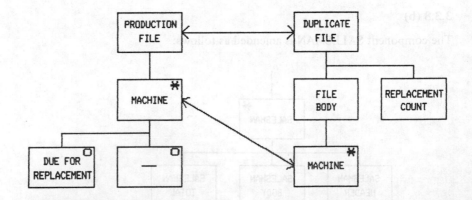

We could have shown MACHINE of the DUPLICATE FILE as a selection of DUE FOR REPLACEMENT or NOT. Since the records are copied across, both possibilities do appear on the output file.

4.3.1 (b)

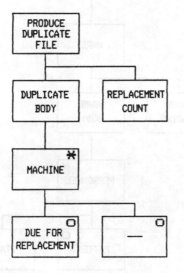

4.3.2

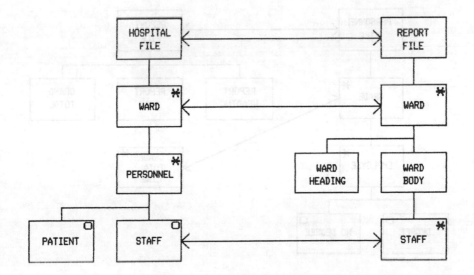

Giving the program structure:

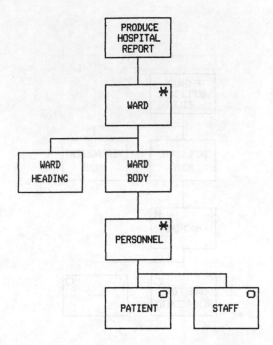

4.3.3 (a) and (b)

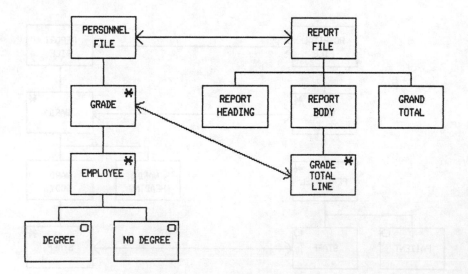

4.3.3 (c)

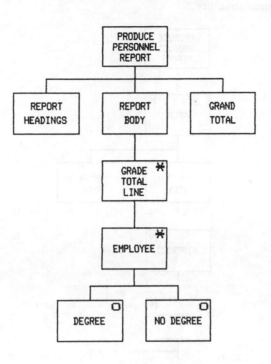

4.3.4

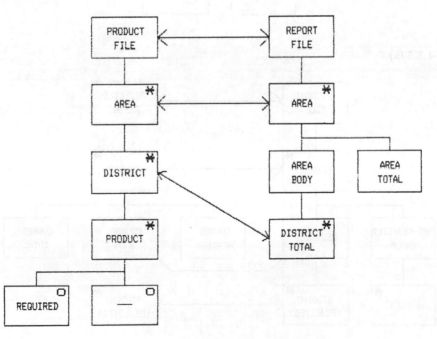

Hence the program structure:

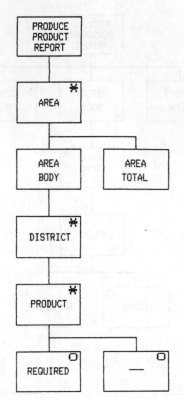

4.3.5 (a)

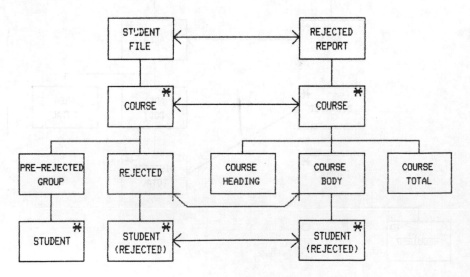

Which when combined give the following program structure:

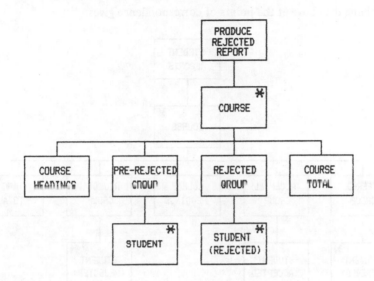

4.3.5 (b)

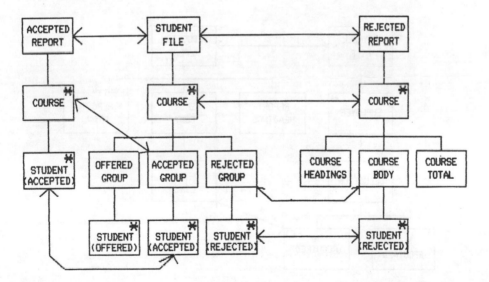

Combining the above at the points of correspondence gives:

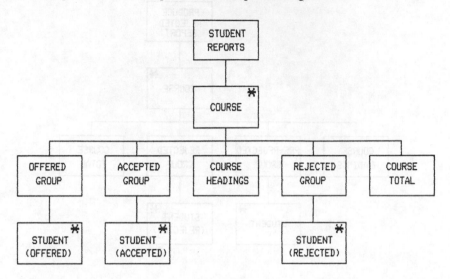

4.3.6 (a) and (b)

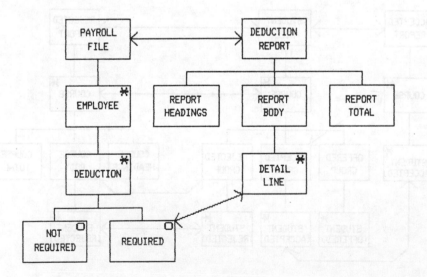

4.3.6 (c)

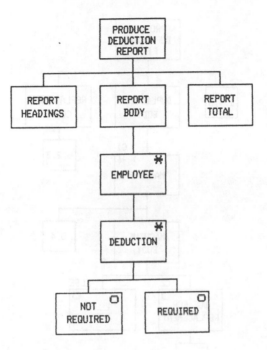

Chapter 5

5.4.1 (a)

C1 – Until end of the input file
C2 – If machine due for replacement

1. Open files
2. Close files
3. Stop
4. Read a machine record
5. Copy a machine record to output
6. Write the count record
7. Increment replacement count
8. Initialise replacement count

5.4.1 (b)–(d)

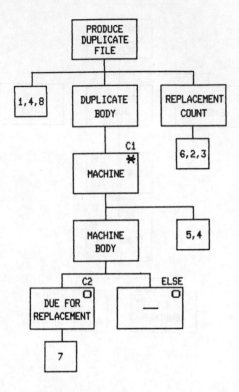

5.4.2 (a)

C1 – Until end of the input file
C2 – Until change of ward or end of the input file
C3 – If person is a patient

1. Open files
2. Close files
3. Stop
4. Read a hospital file record
5. Print ward headings
6. Print staff name
7. Store ward

5.4.2 (b)–(d)

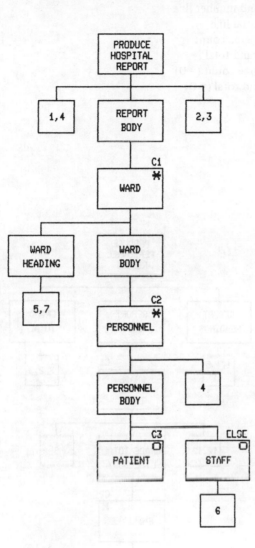

5.4.3 (a)

C1 – Until end of the input file
C2 – Until change of grade or end of the input file
C3 – If degree = 'Y'

1. Open files
2. Close files
3. Stop
4. Read a personnel file record
5. Print report headings

6. Print grade and number line
7. Print grand total line
8. Increment degree count
9. Increment grand total
10. Initialise degree count (= 0)
11. Initialise grand total (= 0)
12. Store grade

5.4.3 (b)–(d)

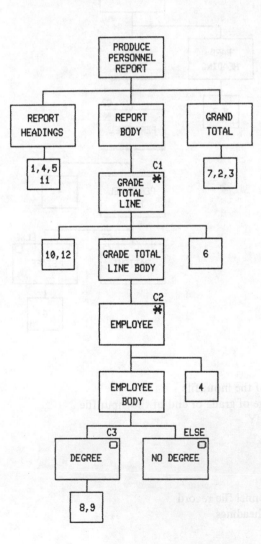

5.4.4 (a)

C1 – Until end of the input file
C2 – Until change of area or end of the input file
C3 – Until change of district or change of area or end of the input file
C4 – If product code is a required one

1. Open files
2. Close files
3. Stop
4. Read a product file record
5. Print area total line
6. Print district total line
7. Add selected value to area total
8. Add selected value to district total
9. Initialise area total
10. Initialise district total
11. Store area code
12. Store district code

5.4.4 (b)–(d)

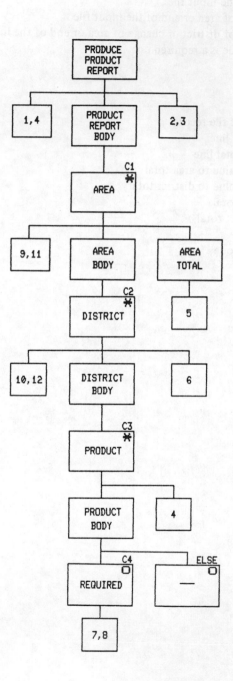

5.4.5 (a)

C1 — Until end of the input file
C2 — Until end of offered group or change of course or end of the input file
C3 — Until end of accepted group or change of course or end of the input file
C4 — Until change of course or end of the input file

1. Open files
2. Close files
3. Stop
4. Read a student file record
5. Print reject report headings
6. Print rejected student name
7. Print reject total
8. Write accepted student record
9. Increment reject total
10. Initialise reject total
11. Store course code

5.4.5 (b)–(d)

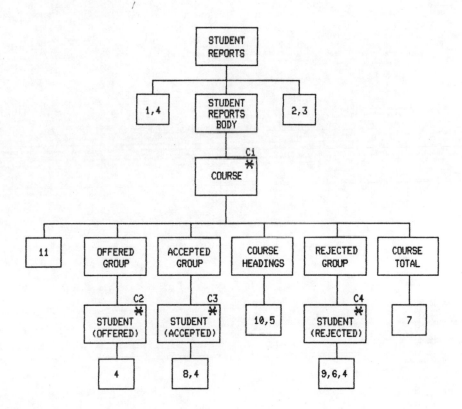

5.4.6 (a)

C1 – Until end of the input file
C2 – Until end of deduction group
C3 – If not (deduction code 20 and amount > £1)

1. Open files
2. Close files
3. Stop
4. Read a payroll file record
5. Print report headings
6. Print name and amount line
7. Print total line
8. Add deduction amount to total
9. Initialise total (= 0)
10. Initialise deduction counter
11. Increment deduction counter

5.4.6 (b)–(d)

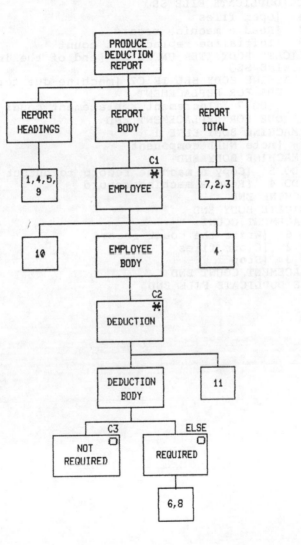

6.3.1

```
PRODUCE DUPLICATE FILE SEQ
   DO 1  [Open files
   DO 4  [Read a machine record
   DO 8  [Initialise replacement count
   DUPLICATE BODY ITER UNTIL C1 [end of the input file
      MACHINE SEQ
         MACHINE BODY SEL IF C2 [machine due for replacement
            DUE FOR REPLACEMENT
               DO 7  [Increment replacement count
            DUE FOR REPLACEMENT END
         MACHINE BODY ELSE 1
            [note NULL component
         MACHINE BODY END
         DO 5  [Copy a machine record to output
         DO 4  [Read a machine record
      MACHINE END
   DUPLICATE BODY END
   REPLACEMENT COUNT
      DO 6  [Write the count record
      DO 2  [Close files
      DO 3  [Stop
   REPLACEMENT COUNT END
PRODUCE DUPLICATE FILE END
```

6.3.2

```
PRODUCE HOSPITAL REPORT SEQ
   DO 1  [Open files
   DO 4  [Read a hospital file record
   REPORT BODY ITER UNTIL C1 [end of the input file
      WARD SEQ
         WARD HEADING
            DO 5  [Print ward headings
            DO 7  [Store ward
         WARD HEADING END
         WARD BODY ITER UNTIL C2 [change of ward or end of the
                                           input file
         PERSONNEL SEQ
            PERSONNEL BODY SEL IF C3 [person is a patient
               PATIENT
                  [note - no operations for this component
               PATIENT END
            PERSONNEL BODY ELSE 1
               STAFF
                  DO 6   [Print staff name
               STAFF END
            PERSONNEL BODY END
            DO 4   [Read a hospital file record
         PERSONNEL END
      WARD BODY END
   WARD END
   REPORT BODY END
   DO 2  [Close files
   DO 3  [Stop
PRODUCE HOSPITAL REPORT END
```

6.3.3

```
PRODUCE PERSONNEL REPORT SEQ
  REPORT HEADINGS
     DO 1   [Open files
     DO 4   [Read a personnel file record
     DO 5   [Print report headings
     DO 11  [Initialise grand total (=0)
  REPORT HEADINGS END
  REPORT BODY ITER UNTIL C1 [end of the input file
     GRADE TOTAL LINE SEQ
        DO 10   [Initialise degree count (=0)
        DO 12   [Store grade
        GRADE TOTAL LINE BODY ITER UNTIL C2 [change of grade
                                        or end of the input file
        EMPLOYEE SEQ
          EMPLOYEE BODY SEL IF C3 [degree = 'Y'
             DEGREE
                DO 8   [Increment degree count
                DO 9   [Increment grand total
             DEGREE END
          EMPLOYEE BODY ELSE 1
             NO DEGREE
                [note - no operations for this component
             NO DEGREE END
          EMPLOYEE BODY END
          DO 4   [Read a personnel file record
        EMPLOYEE END
     GRADE TOTAL LINE BODY END
     DO 6   [Print grade and number line
     GRADE TOTAL LINE END
  REPORT BODY END
  GRAND TOTAL
     DO 7   [Print grand total line
     DO 2   [Close files
     DO 3   [Stop
  GRAND TOTAL END
PRODUCE PERSONNEL REPORT END
```

6.3.4

```
PRODUCE PRODUCT REPORT SEQ
  DO 1   [Open files
  DO 4   [Read a product file record
  PRODUCT REPORT BODY ITER UNTIL C1 [end of the input file
    AREA SEQ
      DO 9  [Initialise area total
      DO 11 [Store area code
      AREA BODY ITER UNTIL C2 [change of area or end of the
                                input file
        DISTRICT SEQ
          DO 10  [Initialise district total
          DO 12  [Store district code
          DISTRICT BODY ITER UNTIL C3 [change of district
              or change of area or end of the input file
            PRODUCT SEQ
              PRODUCT BODY SEL IF C4 [product code is a
                                      required one
                REQUIRED
                  DO 7  [Add selected value to area total
                  DO 8  [Add selected value to district total
                REQUIRED END
              PRODUCT BODY ELSE 1
                [note NULL component
              PRODUCT BODY END
              DO 4   [Read a product file record
            PRODUCT END
          DISTRICT BODY END
          DO 6   [Print district total line
        DISTRICT END
      AREA BODY END
      AREA TOTAL
        DO 5  [Print area total line
      AREA TOTAL END
    AREA END
  PRODUCT REPORT BODY END
  DO 2  [Close files
  DO 3  [Stop
PRODUCE PRODUCT REPORT END
```

6.3.5

```
STUDENT REPORTS SEQ
   DO 1  [Open files
   DO 4  [Read a student file record
   STUDENT REPORTS BODY ITER UNTIL C1 [end of the input file
      COURSE SEQ
         DO 11 [Store course code
         OFFERED GROUP ITER UNTIL C2 [end of offered group or
                      change of course or end of the input file
            STUDENT (OFFERED)
               DO 4  [Read a student file record
            STUDENT (OFFERED) END
         OFFERED GROUP END
         ACCEPTED GROUP ITER UNTIL C3 [end of accepted group
                      or change of course or end of the input file
            STUDENT (ACCEPTED)
               DO 8  [Write accepted student record
               DO 4  [Read a student file record
            STUDENT (ACCEPTED) END
         ACCEPTED GROUP END
         COURSE HEADINGS
            DO 10 [Initialise reject total
            DO 5  [Print reject report headings
         COURSE HEADINGS END
         REJECTED GROUP ITER UNTIL C4 [change of course or end
                                        of the input file
            STUDENT (REJECTED)
               DO 9  [Increment reject total
               DO 6  [Print rejected student name
               DO 4  [Read a student file record
            STUDENT (REJECTED) END
         REJECTED GROUP END
         COURSE TOTAL
            DO 7  [Print reject total
         COURSE TOTAL END
      COURSE END
   STUDENT REPORTS BODY END
   DO 2  [Close files
   DO 3  [Stop
STUDENT REPORTS END
```

6.3.6

```
PRODUCE DEDUCTION REPORT SEQ
  REPORT HEADINGS
    DO 1  [Open files
    DO 4  [Read a payroll file record
    DO 5  [Print report headings
    DO 9  [Initialise total (=0)
  REPORT HEADINGS END
  REPORT BODY ITER UNTIL C1 [end of the input file
    EMPLOYEE SEQ
      DO 10 [Initialise deduction counter
      EMPLOYEE BODY ITER UNTIL C2 [end of deduction group
        DEDUCTION SEQ
          DEDUCTION BODY SEL IF C3 [not (deduction code = 20
                                       and amount > £1)
            NOT REQUIRED
              [note no operations
            NOT REQUIRED END
          DEDUCTION BODY ELSE 1
            REQUIRED
              DO 6  [Print name and amount line
              DO 8  [Add deduction amount to total
            REQUIRED END
          DEDUCTION BODY END
          DO 11 [Increment deduction counter
        DEDUCTION END
      EMPLOYEE BODY END
      DO 4  [Read a payroll file record
    EMPLOYEE END
  REPORT BODY END
  REPORT TOTAL
    DO 7  [Print total line
    DO 2  [Close files
    DO 3  [Stop
  REPORT TOTAL END
PRODUCE DEDUCTION REPORT END
```

7.5.1

```
00100 REM ** produce duplicate file seq **
00110    OPEN "PRODFILE.INP" FOR INPUT AS FILE #1
00120    OPEN "DUPFILE.OUT" FOR OUTPUT AS FILE #2
00130    INPUT #1,RECTYPE%,MACHINE$,DATEPURCH$,REPDUE%
00140    REPCOUNT% = 0
00150    REM ** duplicate body iter **
00160       IF RECTYPE% = 9 GOTO 310
00170       REM ** machine seq **
00180          REM ** machine body sel **
00190             IF NOT (REPDUE% = 9) GOTO 240
00200             REM ** due for replacement **
00210                REPCOUNT% = REPCOUNT% + 1
00220             REM ** due for replacement end **
00230                GOTO 260
00240          REM ** machine body else 1 **
00250             REM ** null component **
00260          REM ** machine body end **
00270          PRINT #2,RECTYPE%;MACHINE$;DATEPURCH$;REPDUE%
00280          INPUT #1,RECTYPE%,MACHINE$,DATEPURCH$,REPDUE%
00290       REM ** machine end **
00300       GOTO 150
00310    REM ** duplicate body end **
00320    REM ** replacement count **
00330       PRINT #2,8;REPCOUNT%
00340       PRINT #2,RECTYPE%;MACHINE$;DATEPURCH$;REPDUE%
00350       CLOSE #1,#2
00360       STOP
00370    REM ** replacement count end **
00380 REM ** produce duplicate file end **
```

7.5.2

```
00100    PROGRAM HOSP1TAL (HOSPFILE,STAFFILE) ;
00200
00300    TYPE
00400       PACKED4 =            PACKED ARRAY [1..4] OF CHAR ;
00500       RECORDTYPE =
00600          RECORD
00700             WARD        : PACKED4 ;
00800             NAME        : PACKED ARRAY [1..20] OF CHAR ;
00900             PATIENT     : BOOLEAN ;
01000          END ;
01100
01200    VAR
```

```
01300         STOREDWARD        : PACKED4 ;
01400         HOSPRECORD        : RECORDTYPE ;
01500         HOSPFILE          : FILE OF RECORDTYPE ;
01600         STAFFILE          : TEXT ;
01700
01800      (* produce hospital report seq *)
01900      BEGIN
02000        RESET (HOSPFILE) ;
02100        REWRITE (STAFFILE) ;
02200        READ (HOSPFILE,HOSPRECORD) ;
02300        WITH HOSPRECORD DO
02400        (* report body iter *)
02500        WHILE NOT (WARD = 'ZZZZ') DO
02600        BEGIN
02700          (* ward seq *)
02800            (* ward heading *)
02900              WRITELN (STAFFILE,'STAFF ON WARD ',WARD) ;
03000              WRITELN (STAFFILE) ;
03100              STOREDWARD := WARD ;
03200            (* ward heading end *)
03300            (* ward body iter *)
03400            WHILE NOT ((WARD = 'ZZZZ') OR
03450                       (WARD <> STOREDWARD)) DO
03500            BEGIN
03600              (* personnel seq *)
03700                (* personnel body sel *)
03800                IF PATIENT THEN
03900                  (* patient *)
04000                    (* no operations for this component *)
04100                  (* patient end *)
04200                (* personnel body else 1 *)
04300                ELSE
04400                  (* staff *)
04500                    WRITELN (STAFFILE,NAME) ;
04600                  (* staff end *)
04700                (* personnel body end *)
04800                READ (HOSPFILE,HOSPRECORD) ;
04900              (* personnel end *)
05000            END ;
05100          (* ward body end *)
05200        (* ward end *)
05300        END ;
05400        (* report body end *)
05500      END.
05600      (* produce hospital report end *)
```

```
00100     IDENTIFICATION DIVISION.
00200     PROGRAM-ID. PERSON.
00300     ENVIRONMENT DIVISION.
00400     INPUT-OUTPUT SECTION.
00500     FILE-CONTROL.
00600         SELECT PERSONNEL-FILE ASSIGN TO DSK.
00700         SELECT OUTPUT-REPORT-FILE ASSIGN TO DSK.
00800     DATA DIVISION.
00900     FILE SECTION.
01000     FD  PERSONNEL-FILE
01100         RECORDING MODE IS ASCII
01200         VALUE OF ID "PERSONSEQ".
01300     01  PERSONNEL-REC.
01400         03  GRADE              PIC 999.
01500         03  NAME               PIC X(17).
01600         03  O-LEVELS           PIC 9.
01700         03  A-LEVELS           PIC 9.
01800         03  DEGREE-Y-N         PIC X.
01900             88  HAS-DEGREE     VALUE "Y".
02000     FD  OUTPUT-REPORT-FILE
02100         RECORDING MODE IS ASCII
02200         VALUE OF ID "REPORTLPT".
02300     01  PRINT-LINE             PIC X(80).
02400     WORKING-STORAGE SECTION.
02500     01  MAIN-HEADINGS          PIC X(36) VALUE
02600         "XYZ COMPANY - EMPLOYEES WITH DEGREES".
02700     01  SUB-HEADINGS           PIC X(36) VALUE
02800         "  GRADE            NUMBER".
02900     01  DETAIL-LINE.
03000         03  FILLER             PIC XX     VALUE SPACES.
03100         03  OUT-GRADE          PIC ZZ9.
03200         03  FILLER             PIC X(15)  VALUE SPACES.
03300         03  OUT-DEGREE-COUNT   PIC ZZZ9.
03400     01  TOTAL-LINE.
03500         03  FILLER             PIC X(19)  VALUE "TOTAL".
03600         03  OUT-GRAND-TOTAL-COUNT PIC ZZZZ9.
03700     77  DEGREE-COUNT           PIC 9(4).
03800     77  GRAND-TOTAL-COUNT      PIC 9(5).
03900     77  STORED-GRADE           PIC 999.
04000     PROCEDURE DIVISION.
04100     PRODUCE-PERSONNEL-REPORT-SEQ.
04200     REPORT-HEADINGS.
04300         OPEN INPUT PERSONNEL-FILE
04400              OUTPUT OUTPUT-REPORT-FILE.
04500         READ PERSONNEL-FILE AT END MOVE 999 TO GRADE.
04600         WRITE PRINT-LINE FROM MAIN-HEADINGS
04700         WRITE PRINT-LINE FROM SUB-HEADINGS AFTER 1
04800         WRITE PRINT-LINE FROM SPACES AFTER 1.
04900         MOVE ZERO TO GRAND-TOTAL-COUNT.
05000     REPORT-HEADINGS-END.
05100     REPORT-BODY-ITER.
05200         IF GRADE = 999
05300             GO TO REPORT-BODY-END.
05400     GRADE-TOTAL-LINE-SEQ.
05500         MOVE ZERO TO DEGREE-COUNT.
05600         MOVE GRADE TO STORED-GRADE.
05700     GRADE-TOTAL-LINE-BODY-ITER.
05800         IF GRADE = 999 OR GRADE NOT = STORED-GRADE
05900             GO TO GRADE-TOTAL-LINE-BODY-END.
06000     EMPLOYEE-SEQ.
```

```
06100     EMPLOYEE-BODY-SEL.
06200         IF HAS-DEGREE
06300             NEXT SENTENCE
06400         ELSE
06500             GO TO EMPLOYEE-BODY-ELSE-1.
06600     DEGREE.
06700         ADD 1 TO DEGREE-COUNT.
06800         ADD 1 TO GRAND-TOTAL-COUNT.
06900     DEGREE-END.
07000         GO TO EMPLOYEE-BODY-END.
07100     EMPLOYEE-BODY-ELSE-1.
07200     NO-DEGREE.
07300     *   NO OPERATIONS FOR THIS COMPONENT
07400     NO-DEGREE-END.
07500     EMPLOYEE-BODY-END.
07600         READ PERSONNEL-FILE AT END MOVE 999 TO GRADE.
07700     EMPLOYEE-END.
07800         GO TO GRADE-TOTAL-LINE-BODY-ITER.
07900     GRADE-TOTAL-LINE-BODY-END.
08000         MOVE STORED-GRADE TO OUT-GRADE
08100         MOVE DEGREE-COUNT TO OUT-DEGREE-COUNT
08200         WRITE PRINT-LINE FROM DETAIL-LINE.
08300     GRADE-TOTAL-LINE-END.
08400         GO TO REPORT-BODY-ITER.
08500     REPORT-BODY-END.
08600     GRAND-TOTAL.
08700         MOVE GRAND-TOTAL-COUNT TO OUT-GRAND-TOTAL-COUNT
08800         WRITE PRINT-LINE FROM TOTAL-LINE.
08900         CLOSE PERSONNEL-FILE OUTPUT-REPORT-FILE.
09000         STOP RUN.
09100     GRAND-TOTAL-END.
09200     PRODUCE-PERSONNEL-REPORT-END.
```

Chapter 8

8.4.1

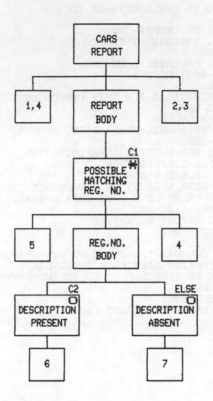

C1 — Until end of CARS SOLD file
C2 — If record found in CARS FOR SALE file (direct access)

1. Open files
2. Close files
3. Stop
4. Read a CARS SOLD file record
5. Attempt to access CARS FOR SALE file record with registration number = that in CARS SOLD file record
6. Print car description
7. Print 'description not known'

8.4.2

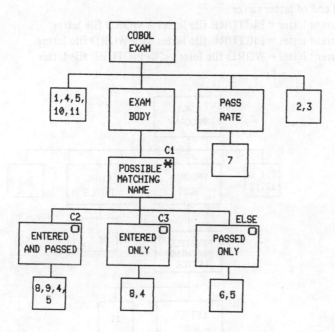

C1 – Until end of both input files
C2 – If ENTERED name = PASSED name
C3 – If ENTERED name < PASSED name

1. Open files
2. Close files
3. Stop
4. Read ENTERED file record
5. Read PASSED file record
6. Print passed/not entered name
7. Compute and print pass rate
8. Increment entered count
9. Increment passed count
10. Initialise entered count
11. Initialise passed count

8.4.3

C1 — Until end of letter range
C2 — If current letter = PICTURE file letter = WORD file letter
C3 — If current letter = PICTURE file letter < > WORD file letter
C4 — If current letter = WORD file letter < > PICTURE file letter

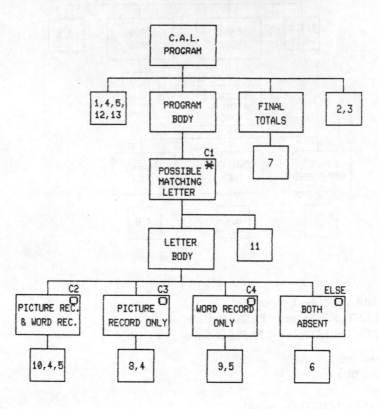

1. Open files
2. Close files
3. Stop
4. Read PICTURE file record
5. Read WORD file record
6. Print appropriate initial letter
7. Compute and print percentages
8. Increment picture only total
9. Increment word only total
10. Increment picture with word total
11. Increment current letter (move to next in alphabet)
12. Initialise all totals
13. Initialise current letter (= A)

8.4.4

In this solution we have simplified the component TRANSACTION ERROR. Strictly, it should contain the same structure as that for TRANSACTION BODY. However, the only operation to be allocated to each of the three selection part components would be number 6.

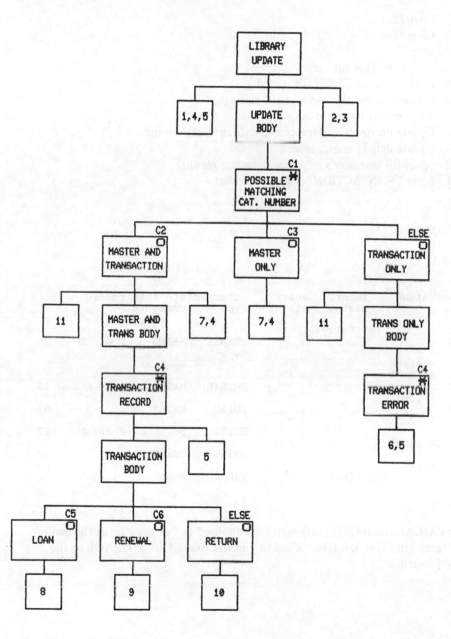

C1 — Until end of both input files
C2 — If MASTER catalogue number = TRANSACTION catalogue number
C3 — If MASTER catalogue number < TRANSACTION catalogue number
C4 — Until change of TRANSACTION catalogue number
C5 — If CODE = 1
C6 — If CODE = 2

1. Open files
2. Close files
3. Stop
4. Read MASTER file record
5. Read TRANSACTION file record
6. Display 'transaction alone' error message
7. Write master record to output
8. Update borrower's reference and date in master record
9. Update date in master record
10. Space-fill borrower's reference in master record
11. Store TRANSACTION catalogue number

Chapter 9

9.7.1

operation	inter. status	entry status	intermediate file type	record contents	
2	0 (False)				
7			DETAIL	MATHS F JONES	35
21					
26 (1st)					
26 (2nd)		2			
7			DETAIL	MATHS C DODD	48
26 (2nd)		2			
8			TOTAL	MATHS	83
26 (2nd)		2			
7			DETAIL	SCIENCE J BROWN	62
26 (2nd)		2			
8			TOTAL	SCIENCE	62
26 (2nd)		2			
4	1 (True)		NULL	NULL	
24					
25					

In PASCAL and BASIC, entry status is initialised to 1 at the start of the main program. In COBOL it is initialised to 1 in the WORKING-STORAGE of the subprogram.

9.7.2 (a)

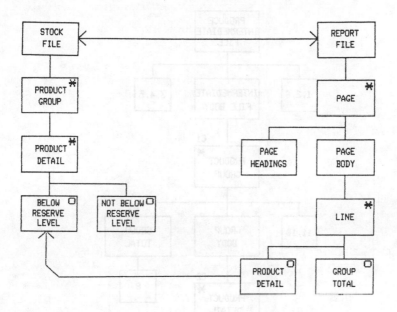

A structure clash exists between PRODUCT GROUP and PAGE.

9.7.2 (b)

Data structures (program 1):

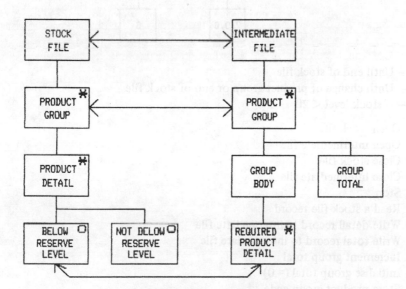

Program structure (program 1):

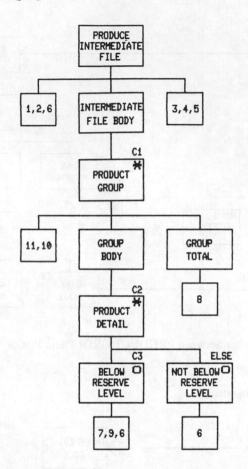

C1 — Until end of stock file
C2 — Until change of product group or end of stock file
C3 — If stock level < 20

1. Open stock file
2. Open intermediate file
3. Close stock file
4. Close intermediate file
5. Stop
6. Read a stock file record
7. Write detail record to intermediate file
8. Write total record to intermediate file
9. Increment group total
10. Initialise group total (= 0)
11. Store product group code

9.7.2 (c)

Data structures (program 2):

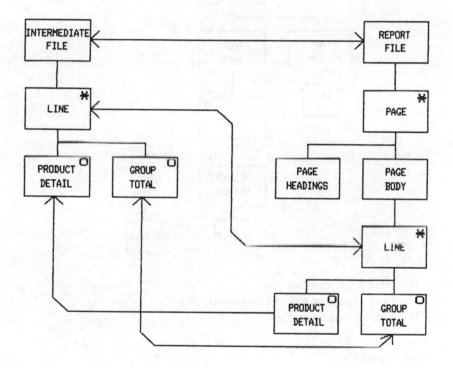

Program structure (program 2):

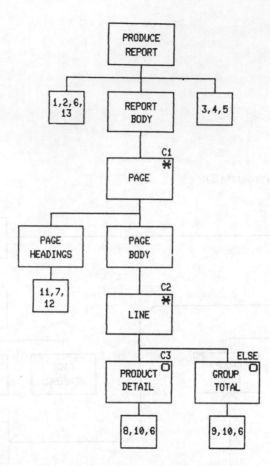

C1 – Until end of intermediate file
C2 – Until end of page or end of intermediate file
C3 – If a product detail line

1. Open intermediate file
2. Open report file
3. Close report file
4. Close intermediate file
5. Stop
6. Read an intermediate file record
7. Print page headings
8. Print detail line
9. Print total line
10. Increment line count

11. Increment page count
12. Initialise line count (= 0)
13. Initialise page count (= 0)

9.7.2 (d)

Use the rules from section 9.5 to code operations 2, 4, 7 and 8 from program 1, and operations 1, 4, 5 and 6 from program 2.

Initialise entry status and include code at the beginning of program 2 for the control passing mechanism.

Chapter 10

10.7.1

```
TABLE SEQ
   DO 9  [Initialise index
   TABLE BODY ITER (? condition)
      ELEMENT SEL IF C1 [target = current element
         TARGET MATCHED
            DO 6   [Process matched target
            DO 10 [Store description(index)              ** (a) **
            QUIT TABLE BODY ITER
         TARGET MATCHED END
      ELEMENT ELSE 1 IF C2 [target < current element
         TARGET CANNOT BE MATCHED
            DO 7   [Process unmatched target
            QUIT TABLE BODY ITER
         TARGET CANNOT BE MATCHED END
      ELEMENT ELSE 2
         TARGET NOT YET MATCHED
            DO 8   [Increment index
            QUIT TABLE BODY ITER IF C4 [index > maximum    ** (b) **
         TARGET NOT YET MATCHED END
      ELEMENT END
   TABLE BODY END
TABLE END
```

10.7.2

First we give the data structures:

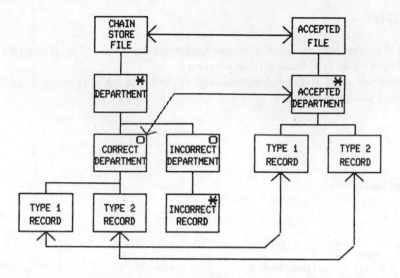

The condition list and operation list follow:

C1 – Until end of chain store file
C2 – Until change of department or end of chain store file

1. Open files
2. Close files
3. Stop
4. Read a chain store file record
5. Write a type 1 record
6. Write a type 2 record
7. Display error message
8. Store department code

The program structure with allocated operations and conditions is:

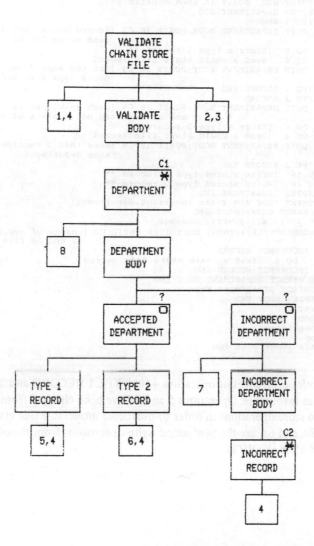

Finally the eventual schematic logic:

```
VALIDATE CHAIN STORE FILE SEQ
   DO 1   [Open files
   DO 4   [Read a chain store file record
   VALIDATE BODY ITER UNTIL C1 [end of chain store file
      DEPARTMENT SEQ
         DO 8   [Store department code
         DEPARTMENT BODY POSIT (A good department)
            ACCEPTED DEPARTMENT SEQ
               TYPE 1 RECORD
                  QUIT DEPARTMENT BODY POSIT IF C3 [record not a type 1 or
                                                   cash value out of range
                  DO 5   [Store a type 1 record **
                  DO 4   [Read a chain store file record
                  QUIT DEPARTMENT BODY POSIT IF C4 [not the same department or
                                                   not a type 2 record
               TYPE 1 RECORD END
               TYPE 2 RECORD
                  QUIT DEPARTMENT BODY POSIT IF C5 [cash value out of range or
                                                   end of day cash not > start of day cash
                  DO 6   [Store a type 2 record **
                  DO 4   [Read a chain store file record
                  QUIT DEPARTMENT BODY POSIT IF C6 [more than 2 records for the
                                                   same department
               TYPE 2 RECORD END
               DO 5A   [Write stored type 1 record **
               DO 6A   [Write stored type 2 record **
            ACCEPTED DEPARTMENT END
         DEPARTMENT BODY ADMIT (An incorrect department)
            INCORRECT DEPARTMENT SEQ
               DO 7   [Display error message
               INCORRECT DEPARTMENT BODY ITER UNTIL C2 [change of department
                                                       or end of file
                  INCORRECT RECORD
                     DO 4   [Read a chain store file record
                  INCORRECT RECORD END
               INCORRECT DEPARTMENT BODY END
            INCORRECT DEPARTMENT END
         DEPARTMENT BODY END
      DEPARTMENT END
   VALIDATE BODY END
   DO 2   [Close files
   DO 3   [Stop
VALIDATE CHAIN STORE FILE END
```

Note that both occurrences of operation 4 (in TYPE 1 RECORD and TYPE 2 RECORD) are favourable. Operations 5 and 6 have been changed from write operations to store operations in order to overcome intolerable side effects. Operations 5A and 6A are the postponed write operations (from stored areas), implemented after all QUITs.

Chapter 12

12.6.1

The menu selection process program structure:

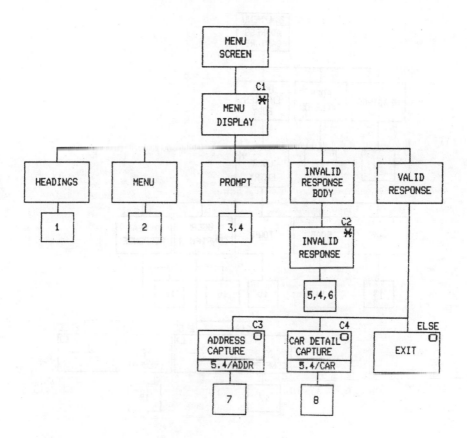

C1 – Until user chooses 'exit'
C2 – Until a valid response
C3 – If user chooses 'address details'
C4 – If user chooses 'car details'

1. Display headings on clear screen
2. Display menu lines
3. Display selection prompt
4. Accept user response
5. Display error message (try again)
6. Clear error message
7. Call address capture subprogram (see below)
8. Call car details capture subprogram (see below)

To implement QUIT from iteration at the schematic logic stage: remove condition C1 from the head of the iteration MENU SCREEN, then allocate QUIT MENU SCREEN ITER to the component EXIT.

The address capture process program structure:

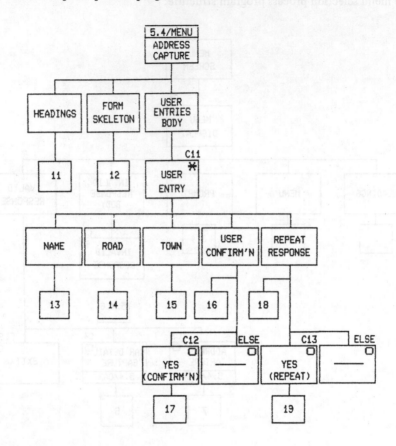

C11 — Until end of user entries
    (that is, until repeat response < > 'Y')
C12 — If user confirmation affirmative
C13 — If repeat response affirmative

11. Display headings on clear screen
12. Display form skeleton
13. Accept name
14. Accept road
15. Accept town
16. Accept user confirmation
17. Write accepted data
18. Accept repeat response
19. Clear form entries

To implement a QUIT out of iteration: remove C11 from the head of the iteration USER ENTRIES BODY and allocate QUIT USER ENTRIES BODY ITER to the ELSE component of REPEAT RESPONSE.

The car details capture process program structure:

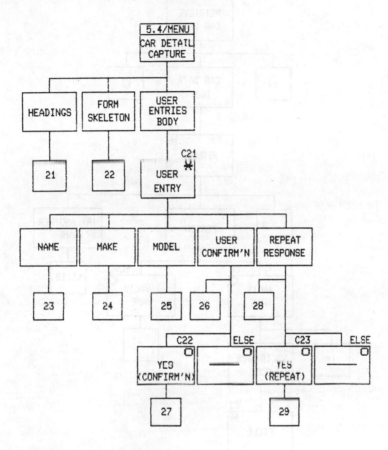

C21 – Until end of user requests
     (that is, until repeat response < > 'Y')
C22 – If user confirmation affirmative
C23 – If repeat response affirmative

21. Display headings on clear screen
22. Display form skeleton
23. Accept name
24. Accept make
25. Accept model
26. Accept user confirmation
27. Write accepted data
28. Accept repeat response
29. Clear form entries

Again we may employ QUIT from iteration in a similar manner to that described for the address capture subprogram.

12.6.2

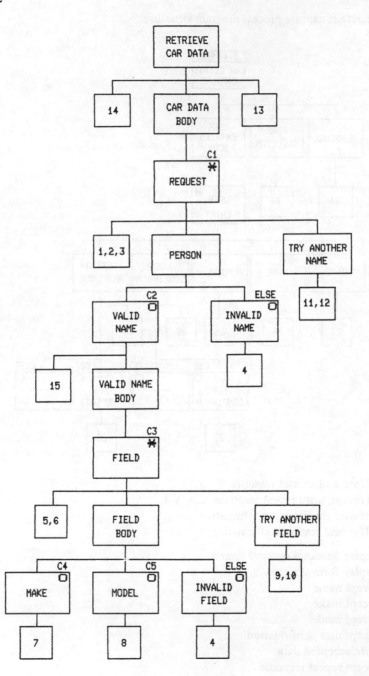

C1 – Until user requests no more (another name response <> 'Y')
C2 – If record for required name found (that is, valid)
C3 – Until user requests no more (another field response <> 'Y')
C4 – If field = 'MAKE'
C5 – If field = 'MODEL'

1. Display 'which person?' prompt
2. Accept user response (name)
3. Attempt to retrieve required record
4. Display 'does not exist'
5. Display 'which field?' prompt
6. Accept user response (field name)
7. Display make of car
8. Display model of car
9. Display 'try another field' prompt
10. Accept user response (another field)
11. Display 'try another name' prompt
12. Accept user response (another name)
13. Display 'exit'
14. Initialise another name response = Y
15. Initialise another field response = Y

Chapter 13

13.4.1

The expected results are:
    Headings for ward A100
    Staff name B C WHITE
    Headings for ward B300
    Staff name A B GREEN

OPERATIONS/ CONDITIONS	WARD	CURRENT RECORD NAME	P/S	STORED WARD	OUTPUT (RESULTS)
1					
4	A100	J G SMITH	P		
C1 (false)					
5					✓
7				A100	
C2 (false)					
C3 (true)					
4	A100	J L THOMAS	P		
C2 (false)					
C3 (true)					
4	A100	B C WHITE	S		
C2 (false)					
C3 (false)					
6					✓
4	B300	A B GREEN	S		
C2 (true)					
C1 (false)					
5					✓
7				B300	
C2 (false)					
C3 (false)					
6					✓
4	--	END OF FILE	--		
C2 (true)					
C1 (true)					
2					
3					

13.4.2

The expected results are:

   Present on both 2, A only 1, B only 0

OPERATIONS/ CONDITIONS	A RECORD	B RECORD	A ONLY COUNT	B ONLY COUNT	BOTH COUNT	OUTPUT (RESULTS)
1						
4	1235					
5		1468				
12			0	0	0	
C1 (false)						
C2 (false)						
C3 (true)						
8				1		
4	1468					
C1 (false)						
C2 (true)						
7					1	
4	1532					
5		1532				
C1 (false)						
C2 (true)						
7					2	
4	9999					
5		9999				
C1 (true)						
6						✓
2						
3						

The test data are insufficient because the ELSE path of the selection PROCESS KEY has not been used and hence operations 9 and 5 of the elementary component FILE B ONLY have not been tested.

Appendix B: An Invoice Printing Case Study

B.1 Objectives

To print invoices from a sales invoice file — see figure B.1. A single customer may have one invoice, or one invoice with one or more extension invoices.

Figure B.1

B.2 Problem description

1. It is required to print invoices from a single sales invoice file. The file is structured such that there may be any number of sales detail records following each customer details record. There may be more than one invoice to be printed per customer but, where it is necessary to print more than one invoice, the extension invoice(s) are identified by customer name only.
2. The sales details for each customer are in individual records (see SALES RECORD — figure B.2) following a record containing a customer's name and address (see CUSTOMER RECORD — figure B.3).
3. Each invoice can hold a maximum of 10 sales detail lines. If there are more than 10 sales details for a customer, extension invoices are produced. The extended invoices will contain a carried forward total, the extension invoices a brought forward total. The final invoice for a customer has a grand total. See figures B.4 and B.5 for samples of an extended first invoice and a final extension invoice.

```
              SALES RECORD
              ------------

CUSTOMER NUMBER         4 digits
PRODUCT DESCRIPTION     30 characters
PRICE                   6 digits (including 2 dec. places)
```

Figure B.2

CUSTOMER RECORD

CUSTOMER NUMBER	4 digits
NAME	20 characters
STREET	20 characters
TOWN	20 characters
COUNTY	20 characters

Figure B.3

```
  1     5      10      15      20      25      30      35      40
P.J.PRENDERGAST LTD.,
MARKET GARDENS,
APPLE TERRACE,
LONDON WC1 3AS

30 BAGS GROW MORE MANURE                    50.00
12 1KG BONE MEAL                            34.70
15 2KG BONE MEAL                            85.00
10 3KG BONE MEAL                            84.65
20 5KG BONE MEAL                           145.70
20 1KG BULB FIBRE                           74.42
24 2KG BULB FIBRE                          125.50
36 3KG BULB FIBRE                          240.70
18 4KG BULB FIBRE                          192.35
48 5KG BULB FIBRE                          405.63

                      CARRIED FORWARD     1438.65
```

Figure B.4

```
  1     5      10      15      20      25      30      35      40
P.J.PRENDERGAST LTD.,




                      BROUGHT FORWARD     1438.65
9 DOZ MIXED TULIPS                          10.00
12 DOZ RED TULIPS                           15.50










                        GRAND TOTAL       1464.15
```

Figure B.5

Appendix C: A Label Production Case Study

C.1 Objectives

To produce adhesive label sets containing hospital patient identification information — see figure C.1. The number of individual labels per patient varies according to laboratory test categories.

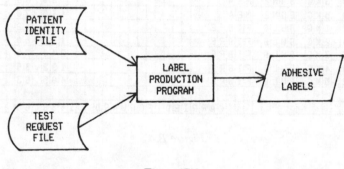

Figure C.1

C.2 Problem description

1. In a hospital system, a file (TEST REQUEST FILE) is created each day, containing records of patients due to enter hospital for laboratory tests. The records contain a patient number and test code, with just one record (that is, test) for each patient. The file is sorted into ascending order of patient number. Another sequential file (PATIENT IDENTITY FILE) is maintained, in patient number order, containing patient identification details (name, age etc.).
2. As both files are sorted into ascending order of patient number, we attempt to match records on the basis of this key field (see figures C.2 and C.3).
3. It is required to produce sets of adhesive labels, such that 3 labels are produced if the test code = 1; 4 labels if the test code = 2; 5 labels otherwise. In the event of patient identification details not being found for a particular test request record, a message is displayed to the computer operator (see figure C.4 for a sample of the labels).

4. The type of label available for printing is self-adhesive on continuous stationery backing, 3 across the page. The program should be easily modifiable to accommodate different types of labels.

```
PATIENT IDENTITY FILE
---------------------

   PATIENT NUMBER       5 digits
   NAME                 15 characters
   AGE                  2 digits
   SEX                  1 character (M or F)
   CONSULTANT           15 characters
```

Figure C.2

```
TEST REQUEST FILE
-----------------

   PATIENT NUMBER       5 digits
   TEST CODE            1 digit
```

Figure C.3

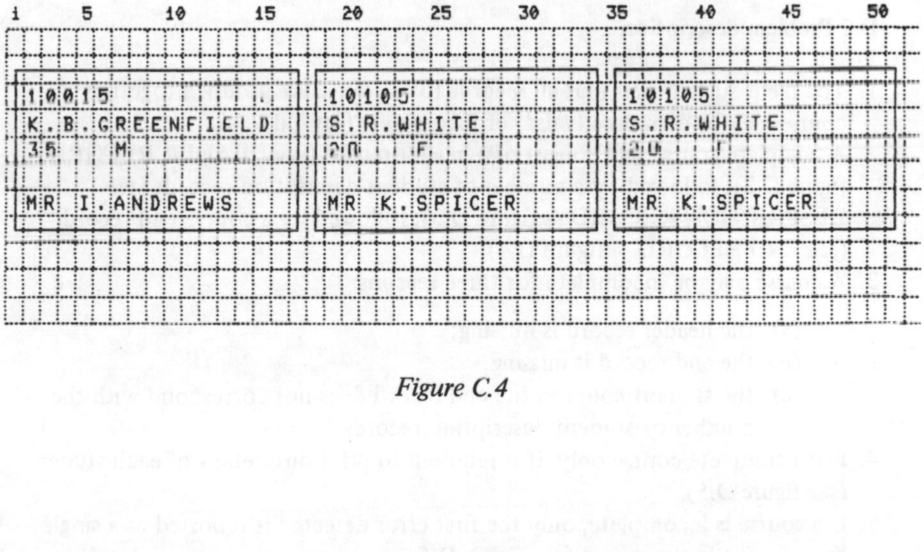

Figure C.4

Appendix D: A Course File Completeness Case Study

D.1 Objectives

To read the course membership file and determine the extent of completeness — see figure D.1.

Figure D.1

D.2 Problem description

1. The file is sorted such that all records for a course are grouped together. A course may be complete (valid) or incomplete (invalid).
2. A complete course will consist of a header record (see HEADER RECORD — figure D.2); followed by a number of student description records (see DESCRIPTION RECORD — figure D.3); followed by a course end record (see END RECORD — figure D.4).
3. A course may be incomplete for three reasons:

      (a) the header record is missing;
  or (b) the end record is missing;
  or (c) the student count in the end record does not correspond with the number of student description records.

4. For a complete course only, it is required to print out details of each student (see figure D.5).
5. If a course is incomplete, only the first error detected is reported as a single line of print in the report (see figure D.5).
6. At the end of the report a summary line is produced showing the number of incomplete courses found (see figure D.5).

```
                        HEADER RECORD
                        -------------

           COURSE CODE        8 characters
           RECORD TYPE        1 character (= A)
```

Figure D.2

```
                     DESCRIPTION RECORD
                     ------------------

           COURSE CODE        8 characters
           RECORD TYPE        1 character (= B)
           STUDENT NAME       15 characters
           ADDRESS            24 characters
```

Figure D.3

```
                         END RECORD
                         ----------

           COURSE CODE        8 characters
           RECORD TYPE        1 character (= E)
           STUDENT COUNT      3 digits
```

Figure D.4

```
  1      5      10     15     20     25     30     35     40     45     50

 COURSE FILE - COMPLETENESS ANALYSIS      12-JAN-85
 ─────────────────────────────────────────────────────

 COURSE    STUDENT NAME        ADDRESS / COMMENT

 BSCASCIV  K.SHERROCKS         ROOM 2, BRYARS HALL
 BSCASCIV  M.WATTERSON         ROOM 7, BRYARS HALL

 BSCASCII                      STUDENT COUNT INCORRECT

 BSCASCI                       HEADER RECORD MISSING

 HNDCSII                       END RECORD MISSING

        **  3 INVALID COURSES FOUND  **
```

Figure D.5

Appendix E: An Interactive System Case Study

E.1 Objectives

To allow the insertion of new contracts to, and the deletion of old contracts from, a microcomputer maintenance contract database. To allow certain interrogation facilities. See figure E.1.

Figure E.1

E.2 Problem description

1. Four facilities are required of the program:
   (a) insert new contract details (see screen layout INSERT NEW CONTRACT – figure E.3);
   (b) delete cancelled contracts (see DELETE CANCELLED CONTRACT – figure E.4);
   (c) view or inspect the details of a given contract (see VIEW CONTRACT DETAILS – figure E.5);
   (d) list all contract details where the cost is high, that is, over £100 per annum (see LIST CONTRACT DETAILS – figure E.6).

   The selection of the required facilities is done by a simple menu (see MENU – figure E.2).
2. The only data validation, except by the user's visual inspection, is when attempts are made to access a contract that does not exist and when an invalid menu choice is made. In such cases an error message is displayed (see figures E.2, E.4 and E.5).
3. The simple database contains, for each contract, a contract number, a model description and the maintenance cost per annum. Facilities of the database management system, which can be incorporated into the program, include the

198

ability to access directly any contract by reference to the contract number, and to find (or locate) all contracts with given attribute values (for example, model = Spectrum 48K, cost > £100) and return the number of records found.

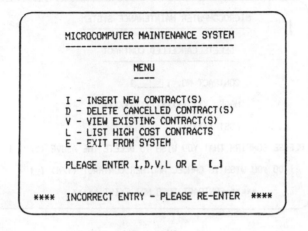

```
          MICROCOMPUTER MAINTENANCE SYSTEM
          -----------------------------------

                         MENU
                         ----

          I - INSERT NEW CONTRACT(S)
          D - DELETE CANCELLED CONTRACT(S)
          V - VIEW EXISTING CONTRACT(S)
          L - LIST HIGH COST CONTRACTS
          E - EXIT FROM SYSTEM

          PLEASE ENTER I,D,V,L OR E  [_]


    ****  INCORRECT ENTRY - PLEASE RE-ENTER  ****
```

Figure E.2

The error message on the bottom line is displayed only after an incorrect entry and is cleared after the user has entered a new value. The user must eventually enter a correct value.

```
          MICROCOMPUTER MAINTENANCE SYSTEM
          -----------------------------------

                 INSERT NEW CONTRACT
                 -------------------

             CONTRACT NO. [_____]

             MODEL [_____]

             COST [____.__] P.A.

    PLEASE CONFIRM THAT THE ABOVE IS CORRECT (Y/N) [_]

    DO YOU WISH TO ENTER ANOTHER NEW CONTRACT (Y/N) [_]
```

Figure E.3

The whole of the above 'form' is displayed on the screen and the user is guided through it. After each response the cursor moves to the next position. The data are written to the database only if user confirmation response is Y. If the user elects to repeat the transaction, the entries on the form, but nothing else, are cleared.

```
        MICROCOMPUTER MAINTENANCE SYSTEM
        --------------------------------

             DELETE CANCELLED CONTRACT
             -------------------------

          CONTRACT NO. [_____]

          MODEL XXXXXXXXXXXXXXXXXXXX

          COST XXXX.XX

PLEASE CONFIRM THAT YOU WISH TO DELETE THE ABOVE (Y/N) [_]

     DO YOU WISH TO CANCEL ANOTHER CONTRACT (Y/N) [_]

          ***** CONTRACT DOES NOT EXIST *****
```

Figure E.4

Headings and the contract number prompt are displayed on a cleared screen. If the user enters a valid contract number, the contract details are displayed and then the user confirmation prompt. The record is deleted only if the confirmation response is Y. The repeat prompt is then displayed. For an invalid contract number, the error message is displayed and then the repeat prompt. If the user elects to delete another contract, the above process is repeated.

```
        MICROCOMPUTER MAINTENANCE SYSTEM
        --------------------------------

             VIEW CONTRACT DETAILS
             ---------------------

          CONTRACT NO. [_____]

          MODEL XXXXXXXXXXXXXXXXXXXX

          COST XXXX.XX


     DO YOU WISH TO VIEW ANOTHER CONTRACT (Y/N) [_]

          ***** CONTRACT DOES NOT EXIST *****
```

Figure E.5

The operation of this screen is similar to the DELETE CANCELLED CONTRACT screen.

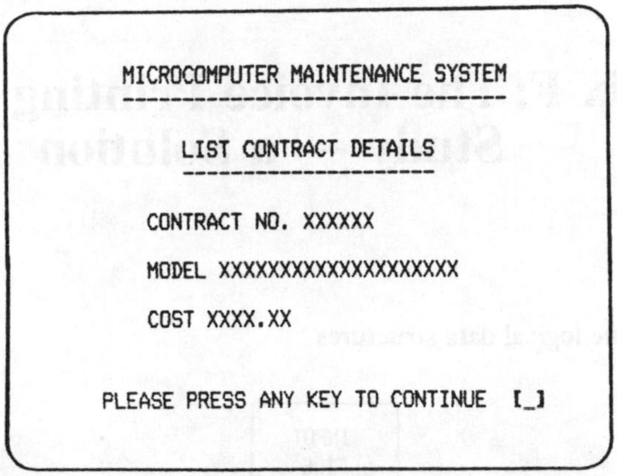

```
┌─────────────────────────────────────────────┐
│                                               │
│     MICROCOMPUTER MAINTENANCE SYSTEM          │
│     ------------------------------            │
│                                               │
│          LIST CONTRACT DETAILS                │
│          ---------------------                │
│                                               │
│      CONTRACT NO. XXXXXX                       │
│                                               │
│      MODEL XXXXXXXXXXXXXXXXXXXX                │
│                                               │
│      COST XXXX.XX                              │
│                                               │
│                                               │
│      PLEASE PRESS ANY KEY TO CONTINUE  [_]    │
│                                               │
└─────────────────────────────────────────────┘
```

Figure E.6

The headings are displayed first. If there are no high cost contracts, the message

NO CONTRACTS FOUND

is displayed in the centre of the screen, and the prompt

PLEASE PRESS ANY KEY TO CONTINUE [_]

is displayed at the bottom of the screen. For each high cost contract, the details and prompt given in figure E.6 are displayed.

Appendix F: The Invoice Printing Case Study — a Solution

F.1 Stage 1 — the logical data structures

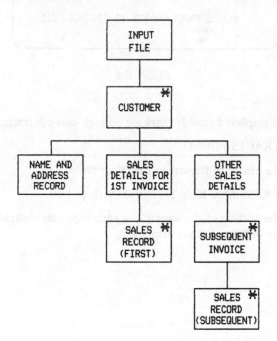

Figure F.1

In respect of the input file (see figure F.1), logically we know that the sales details for each customer may make up more than one invoice, of which the first has special significance in that it will contain full headings. We can reflect this, as shown above, by recognising that each customer has a sequence of a name and address record, followed by the sales detail records, which make up the first invoice, followed by the sales detail records, which make up any subsequent invoices.

The print file (see figure F.2) is also logically concerned with first and subsequent invoices, and also with final and intermediate totals. Note that the carried

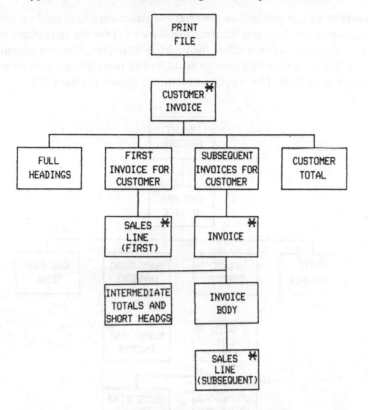

Figure F.2

forward total at the end of an extended invoice, together with the name and brought forward total at the head of the extension invoice, are grouped together as one component INTERMEDIATE TOTALS AND SHORT HEADGS.

F.2 Stage 2 – correspondences and program structure

The correspondences are:

INPUT FILE ⟷ PRINT FILE
CUSTOMER ⟷ CUSTOMER INVOICE
NAME AND ADDRESS RECORD ⟷ FULL HEADINGS
SALES DETAILS FOR 1ST INVOICE ⟷ FIRST INVOICE FOR CUSTOMER
OTHER SALES DETAILS ⟷ SUBSEQUENT INVOICES FOR CUSTOMER
SUBSEQUENT INVOICE ⟷ INVOICE
SALES RECORD (FIRST) ⟷ SALES LINE (FIRST)
SALES RECORD (SUBSEQUENT) ⟷ SALES LINE (SUBSEQUENT)

This leaves three components on the print file structure which have no corresponding components on the input file structure. Two of these are elementary components and as such will not affect the problem structure. The component INVOICE BODY is necessary only to avoid having two different component type parts at the same level. The program structure is shown in figure F.3.

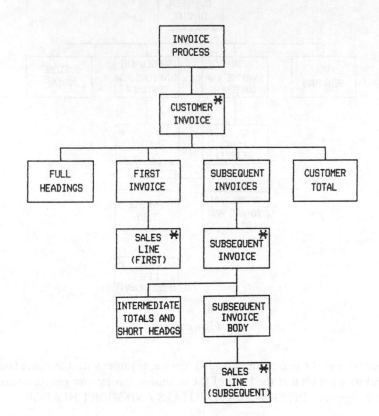

Figure F.3

F.3 Stage 3 — the condition and operation lists

There are four iterations in the program structure; this indicates four conditions, but we can use C2 in two places.

C1 — Until end of input file

C2 — Until change of customer or end of input file or expiration of line count (invoice full)

C3 — Until change of customer or end of input file

The operations are:

1. Open files
2. Close files
3. Stop
4. Read an input file record
5. Print customer name and address at head of form
6. Print grand total
7. Print a sales detail line
8. Print stored customer name at head of form
9. Print brought forward total
10. Print carried forward total
11. Accumulate customer total
12. Store customer name (for short headings)
13. Increment line count
14. Initialise customer total (= 0)
15. Store customer number (to enable C2, C3)
16. Set line count = 0 (to enable C2)

F.4 Stage 4 – allocation of operations and conditions

See figure F.4.

F.5 Stage 5 – the schematic logic

See figure F.5.

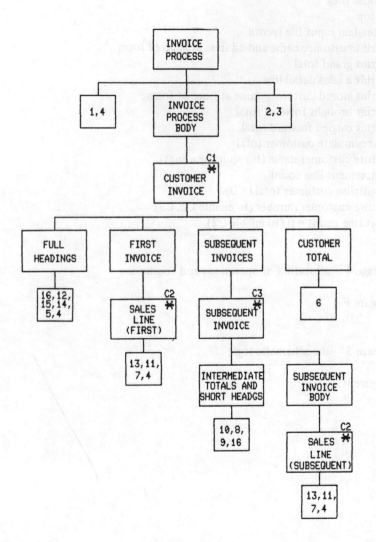

Figure F.4

```
INVOICE PROCESS SEQ
   DO 1   [Open files
   DO 4   [Read an input file record
   INVOICE PROCESS BODY ITER UNTIL C1 [end of input file
      CUSTOMER INVOICE SEQ
         FULL HEADINGS
            DO 16   [Set line count = 0
            DO 12   [Store customer name
            DO 15   [Store customer number
            DO 14   [Initialise customer total
            DO 5    [Print customer name and address at head of form
            DO 4    [Read an input file record
         FULL HEADINGS END
         FIRST INVOICE ITER UNTIL C2 [change of customer or end of
                                input file or expiration of line count
            SALES LINE (FIRST)
               DO 13   [Increment line count
               DO 11   [Accumulate customer total
               DO 7    [Print a sales detail line
               DO 4    [Read an input file record
            SALES LINE (FIRST) END
         FIRST INVOICE END
         SUBSEQUENT INVOICES ITER UNTIL C3 [change of customer or
                                end of input file
            SUBSEQUENT INVOICE SEQ
               INTERMEDIATE TOTALS AND SHORT HEADGS
                  DO 10.  [Print carried forward total
                  DO 8    [Print stored customer name at head of form
                  DO 9    [Print carried forward total
                  DO 16   [Set line count = 0
               INTERMEDIATE TOTALS AND SHORT HEADGS END
               SUBSEQUENT INVOICE BODY ITER UNTIL C2 [change of
               customer or end of input file or expiration of line count
                  SALES LINE (SUBSEQUENT)
                     DO 13   [Increment line count
                     DO 11   [Accumulate customer total
                     DO 7    [Print a sales detail line
                     DO 4    [Read an input file record
                  SALES LINE (SUBSEQUENT) END
               SUBSEQUENT INVOICE BODY END
            SUBSEQUENT INVOICE END
         SUBSEQUENT INVOICES END
         CUSTOMER TOTAL
            DO 6   [Print grand total
         CUSTOMER TOTAL END
      CUSTOMER INVOICE END
   INVOICE PROCESS BODY END
   DO 2   [Close files
   DO 3   [Stop
INVOICE PROCESS END
```

Figure F.5

Appendix G: The Label Production Case Study — a Solution

G.1 Stage 1 – the logical data structures

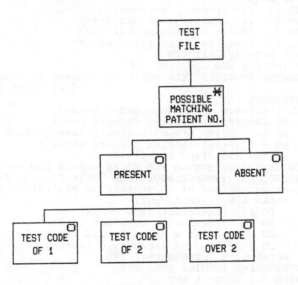

Figure G.1

The test file (see figure G.1) is logically an iteration of possible matching patient number that is either present or absent. If the patient number is present, then it is associated with a test code which has a choice (selection) of three pertinent values.

The patient identity file (see figure G.2) is also an iteration of possible matching patient number which is either present or absent.

Correspondences between the input files are easy to find, and follow the usual course for the merge or collate solution, giving the merged input file structure shown in figure G.3.

The output or label file (see figure G.4) is an iteration of label set, each of which, allowing for the last set, is an iteration of up to three labels.

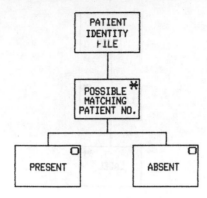

Figure G.2

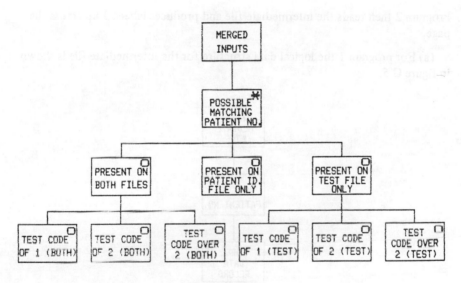

Figure G.3

G.2 Stage 2 – correspondences and program structure

The component MERGED INPUTS obviously corresponds to LABEL FILE, but
there are no more correspondences. Since the labels for a particular patient may
be contained within one label set (of 3) or spread over two label sets, the boundary
of POSSIBLE MATCHING PATIENT NO. clashes with the boundary of LABEL
SET. It is therefore impossible to produce a single program structure.

We solve the problem by designing two separate programs. Program 1 merges
the two input files and produces an intermediate file of records containing the
relevant label data (patient number, name etc.), with one record for each label.

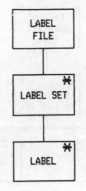

Figure G.4

Program 2 then reads the intermediate file and produces labels, 3 up across the page.

(a) For program 1 the logical data structure for the intermediate file is shown in figure G.5.

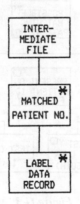

Figure G.5

We can now identify correspondences with the merged input file. MERGED IN-PUTS corresponds with INTERMEDIATE FILE; and PRESENT ON BOTH FILES corresponds with MATCHED PATIENT NO.

Thus the program structure is as shown in figure G.6.

(b) For program 2 the logical data structure for the intermediate file is given in figure G.7.

Correspondences with the output file are now straightforward. LABEL FILE corresponds with INTERMEDIATE FILE and LABEL corresponds with LABEL DATA RECORD.

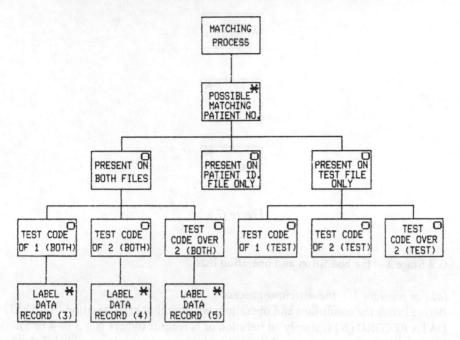

Figure G.6

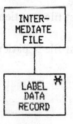

Figure G.7

Thus the program structure is as shown in figure G.8.

After we have completed the design process for the two programs, we can use the technique of inversion to combine the two programs. This involves making one program a subprogram or procedure of the other.

Figure G.8

G.3 Stage 3 – the condition and operation lists

(a) For program 1 – the matching process

Before listing the conditions and operations we note that each iteration of LABEL DATA RECORD (N) is simply an iteration of N records (where N = 3 or 4 or 5). We can therefore remove each of these elementary components, provided that we use elementary operations which write the appropriate number of records.

C1 – Until end of test request file

C2 – If patient number of the test file = patient number of the patient identity file

C3 – If patient number of the test file > patient number of the patient identity file

C4 – If test code = 1

C5 – If test code = 2

1. Open input files
2. Open intermediate file
3. Close input files
4. Close intermediate file
5. Stop
6. Read a test file record
7. Read a patient identity file record
8. Write 3 intermediate file records
9. Write 4 intermediate file records
10. Write 5 intermediate file records
11. Display error message

(b) For program 2 – the label production process

C1 – Until end of intermediate file

C2 — Until end of label set or end of intermediate file

1. Open intermediate file
2. Open label file
3. Close intermediate file
4. Close label file
5. Stop
6. Read an intermediate file record
7. Write a set of labels
8. Construct a label in set (indexed by label subscript)
9. Increment label subscript
10. Set label subscript = 1
11. Initialise a label set (space fill a label set area)

G.4 Stage 4 — allocation of conditions and operations

(a) Program 1 — the matching process
From the problem specification we note that each selection part of PRESENT
ON TEST FILE ONLY generates the same error message. The selection is unnecessary and will therefore be omitted. Thus the program structure is as shown in figure G.9.

(b) Program 2 — the label production process (see figure G.10)

G.5 Stage 5 — the schematic logic

See figures G.11 and G.12.

G.6 Stage 6 — applying the technique of inversion

We shall choose to make the label production process a subprogram of the matching program. This means observing the following when implementing our design in the target language.

For the main program (program 1)
We code

      2. Open intermediate file

by initialising an intermediate file status indicator.
We code

      8, 9 and 10. Write intermediate file records

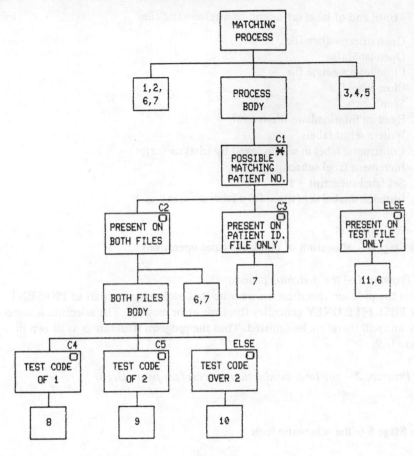

Figure G.9

by calling the subprogram N times and passing the two parameters: the intermediate file record and the intermediate file status indicator.
We code

    4. Close intermediate file

by calling the subprogram with the intermediate file status indicator set to 'end
of file'.

For the subprogram (program 2)
At the start of the subprogram we include code to implement the control passing
mechanism for logical reads.
We code

    1. Open intermediate file

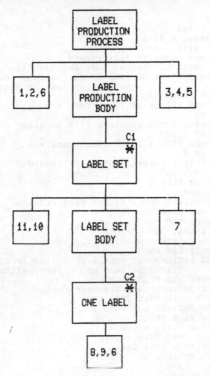

Figure G.10

and the first occurrence of

    6. Read an intermediate file record

by nothing.
We code subsequent occurrences of

    6. Read an intermediate file record

by setting the entry status indicator to a value indicating which occurrence of the 'read' it is, then exiting from the subprogram, then inserting an entry-point label. We code

    3. Close intermediate file

by nothing.
We code

    5. Stop

by code to exit from the subprogram.

```
MATCHING PROCESS SEQ
   DO 1  [Open input files
   DO 2  [Open intermediate file
   DO 6  [Read a test file record
   DO 7  [Read a patient identity file record
   PROCESS BODY ITER UNTIL C1 [End of test request file
      POSSIBLE MATCHING PATIENT NO. SEL IF C2 [Patient no. of the test file
                                    = patient no. of the patient identity file
         PRESENT ON BOTH FILES SEQ
            BOTH FILES BODY SEL IF C4 [Test code = 1
               TEST CODE OF 1
                  DO 8   [Write 3 intermediate file records
               TEST CODE OF 1 END
            BOTH FILES BODY ELSE 1 IF C5 [Test code = 2
               TEST CODE OF 2
                  DO 9   [Write 4 intermediate file records
               TEST CODE OF 2 END
            BOTH FILES BODY ELSE 2
               TEST CODE OVER 2
                  DO 10  [Write 5 intermediate file records
               TEST CODE OVER 2 END
            BOTH FILES BODY END
            DO 6  [Read a test file record
            DO 7  [Read a patient identity file record
         PRESENT ON BOTH FILES END
      POSSIBLE MATCHING PATIENT NO. ELSE 1 IF C3 [Patient no. of the test
                           file > patient no. of the patient identity file
         PRESENT ON PATIENT ID FILE ONLY
            DO 7  [Read a patient identity file record
         PRESENT ON PATIENT ID FILE ONLY END
      POSSIBLE MATCHING PATIENT NO. ELSE 2
         PRESENT ON TEST FILE ONLY
            DO 11  [Display error message
            DO 6   [Read a test file record
         PRESENT ON TEST FILE ONLY END
      POSSIBLE MATCHING PATIENT NO. END
   PROCESS BODY END
   DO 3  [Close input files
   DO 4  [Close intermediate file
   DO 5  [Stop
MATCHING PROCESS END
```

Figure G.11

```
LABEL PRODUCTION PROCESS SEQ
   DO 1  [Open intermediate file
   DO 2  [Open label file
   DO 6  [Read an intermediate file record
   LABEL PRODUCTION BODY ITER UNTIL C1 [End of intermediate file
      LABEL SET SEQ
         DO 11  [Initialise a label set (space fill a label set area)
         DO 10  [Set label subscript = 1
         LABEL SET BODY ITER UNTIL C2 [End of label set or end of
                                       intermediate file
            ONE LABEL
               DO 8  [Construct a label in set(label subscript)
               DO 9  [Increment label subscript
               DO 6  [Read an intermediate file record
            ONE LABEL END
         LABEL SET BODY END
         DO 7  [Write a set of labels
      LABEL SET END
   LABEL PRODUCTION BODY END
   DO 3  [Close intermediate file
   DO 4  [Close label file
   DO 5  [Stop
LABEL PRODUCTION PROCESS END
```

Figure G.12

Appendix H: The Course File Completeness Case Study — a Solution

H.1 Stage 1 – the logical data structures

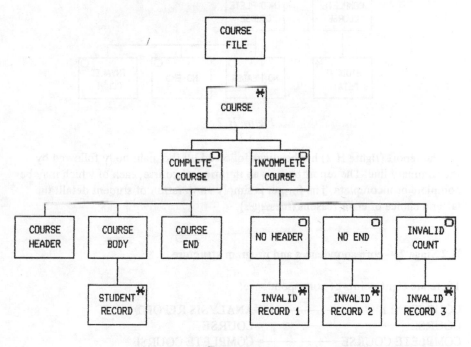

Figure H.1

The course file (figure H.1) is an iteration of course, each of which may be regarded as either complete (valid) or incomplete (invalid). A complete course is a sequence of a header, followed by a body (which is an iteration of student record), followed by an end record. The incomplete course is a selection of the causes of incompleteness, because each cause gives rise to a different error message (that is, no header or no end record or invalid count of students). Each type of incomplete course is an iteration of invalid record.

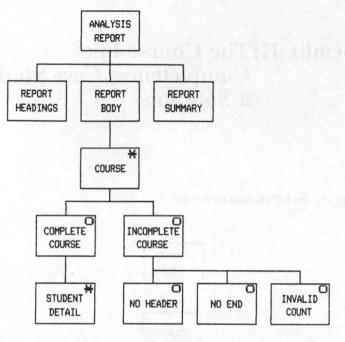

Figure H.2

The report (figure H.2) has headings followed by the main body followed by the summary line. The report body is an iteration of course, each of which may be complete or incomplete. The former is simply an iteration of student detail; the latter a choice of error reasons (messages).

H.2 Stage 2 – correspondences and program structure

There are eight points of correspondence:

COURSE FILE ←——————————→ ANALYSIS REPORT
COURSE ←————————————→ COURSE
COMPLETE COURSE ←————————→ COMPLETE COURSE
INCOMPLETE COURSE ←————————→ INCOMPLETE COURSE
STUDENT RECORD ←———————→ STUDENT DETAIL
NO HEADER ←————————————→ NO HEADER
NO END ←——————————————→ NO END
INVALID COUNT ←————————→ INVALID COUNT

The resultant program structure is shown in figure H.3.

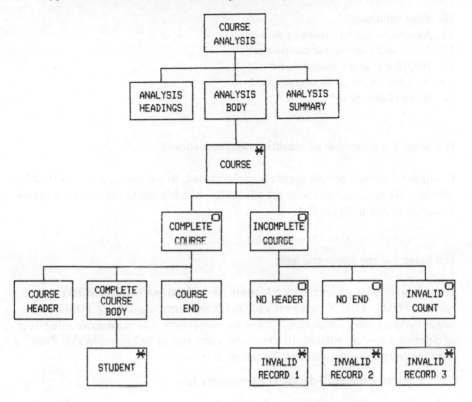

Figure H.3

H.3 Stage 3 – the condition and operation lists

C1 – Until end of course file
C2 – If a complete course!!!
C3 – Until course end record
C4 – If error 'header record missing'
C5 – If error 'end record missing'
C6 – Until change of course or end of file

1. Open files
2. Close files
3. Stop
4. Read a course file record
5. Print analysis heading
6. Print a student's details
7. Print error line 'student count incorrect'
8. Print error line 'header record missing'
9. Print error line 'end record missing'

10. Print summary
11. Increment student record count
12. Increment incomplete course count
13. Initialise student record count
14. Initialise incomplete course count
15. Store course code

H.4 Stage 4 – allocation of conditions and operations

Condition 2 cannot be appropriately implemented, so we recognise a backtracking problem. We will continue with the allocation, which leads to the revised program structure shown in figure H.4.

H.5 Stage 5 – the schematic logic

Having established a backtracking solution, the selection COURSE BODY becomes a POSIT/ADMIT construct and QUITs are introduced in the POSIT component when causes for incompleteness are recognised. The intolerable side effect of printing a student's details (if the course turns out to be incomplete) is dealt with by postponing the printing. Operation 6 becomes

6. Store a student's details in a temporary file

and a new operation must be introduced to accommodate the printing after all QUITs have been passed:

16. Print all student details from the temporary file.

To support operations 6 and 16 we also need:

17. Initialise temporary file.

The revised schematic logic is shown in figure H.5.

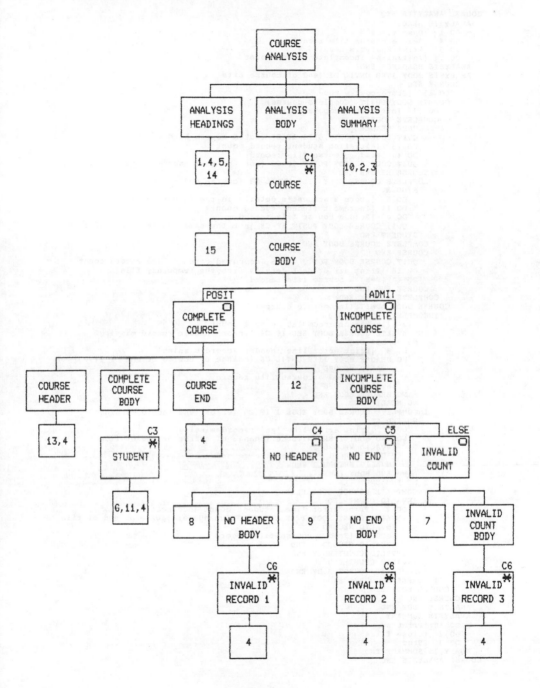

Figure H.4

```
COURSE ANALYSIS SEQ
  ANALYSIS HEADINGS
    DO  1  [Open files
    DO  4  [Read a course file record
    DO  5  [Print analysis heading
    DO 14  [Initialise incomplete course count
  ANALYSIS HEADINGS END
  ANALYSIS BODY ITER UNTIL C1 [end of course file
    COURSE SEQ
      DO 15  [Store course code
      COURSE BODY POSIT (Complete course)
        DO 17  [Initialise temporary file
        COMPLETE COURSE SEQ
          COURSE HEADER
            QUIT COURSE BODY POSIT IF C7 [not a course header
            DO 13  [Initialise student record count
            DO  4  [Read a course file record
            QUIT COURSE BODY POSIT IF C8 [not the same course or end of file
          COURSE HEADER END
          COMPLETE COURSE BODY ITER UNTIL C3 [course end record
            STUDENT
              DO  6  [Store a student's details in the temporary file
              DO 11  [Increment student record count
              DO  4  [Read a course file record
              QUIT COURSE BODY POSIT IF C8 [not the same course or end of file
            STUDENT END
          COMPLETE COURSE BODY END
          COURSE END
            QUIT COURSE BODY POSIT IF C9 [computed count <> end record count
            DO 16  [Print all student details from the temporary file
            DO  4  [Read a course file record
          COURSE END END
        COMPLETE COURSE END
      COURSE BODY ADMIT (Incomplete course)
        INCOMPLETE COURSE SEQ
          DO 12  [Increment incomplete course count
          INCOMPLETE COURSE BODY SEL IF C4 [error 'header record missing'
            NO HEADER SEQ
              DO  8  [Print error line 'header record missing'
              NO HEADER BODY ITER UNTIL C6 [change of course or end of file
                INVALID RECORD 1
                  DO  4  [Read a course file record
                INVALID RECORD 1 END
              NO HEADER BODY END
            NO HEADER END
          INCOMPLETE COURSE BODY ELSE 1 IF C5 [error 'end record missing'
            NO END SEQ
              DO  9  [Print error line 'end record missing'
              NO END BODY ITER UNTIL C6 [change of course or end of file
                INVALID RECORD 2
                  DO  4  [Read a course file record
                INVALID RECORD 2 END
              NO END BODY END
            NO END END
          INCOMPLETE COURSE BODY ELSE 2
            INVALID COUNT SEQ
              DO  7  [Print error line 'student count incorrect'
              INVALID COUNT BODY ITER UNTIL C6 [change of course or end of file
                INVALID RECORD 3
                  DO  4  [Read a course file record
                INVALID RECORD 3 END
              INVALID COUNT BODY END
            INVALID COUNT END
          INCOMPLETE COURSE BODY END
        INCOMPLETE COURSE END
      COURSE BODY END
    COURSE END
  ANALYSIS BODY END
  ANALYSIS SUMMARY
    DO 10  [Print summary
    DO  2  [Close files
    DO  3  [Stop
  ANALYSIS SUMMARY END
COURSE ANALYSIS END
```

Figure H.5

Appendix I: The Interactive System Case Study — a Solution

As we develop the data structure for the menu screen, it becomes apparent that we can best proceed by designing five small processes: a menu driver as the main program and four separate subprograms for the facilities insert, delete, view and list. Furthermore, the simple database, with its direct access facilities, will not influence our design. This means that the structure of each screen becomes the appropriate subprogram structure. The solution is therefore presented in the form of five program structures with allocated operations and conditions.

The program structure for the MENU driver process is first given — see figure I.1.

The operation and condition list is:

C1 — Until user chooses to exit (note that this is implemented by allocating a QUIT from iteration to the component EXIT)
C2 — Until a valid response
C3 — If an insert request
C4 — If a deletion request
C5 — If a view request
C6 — If a list request

1. Initialise (open) database
2. Reset (close) database
3. Stop
4. Accept menu choice
5. Clear screen and display menu skeleton
6. Display error message
7. Clear error message from screen
8. Call insert requests procedure
9. Call deletion requests procedure
10. Call view requests procedure
11. Call list requests procedure

Next we show the INSERT REQUESTS procedure — see figure I.2.
The operation and condition list is:

223

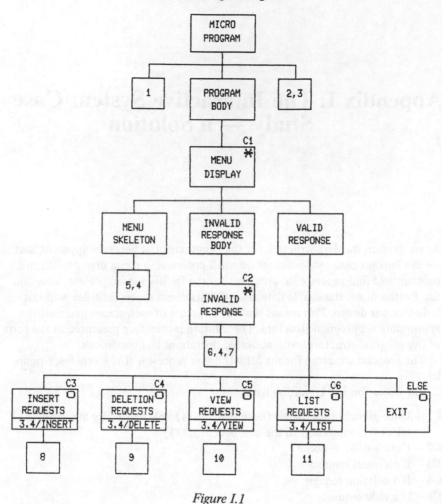

Figure I.1

C11 – Until user no longer requires this option (note that this is implemented by
      allocating a QUIT from iteration to the component REPEAT RESPONSE
      after operation 17)

C12 – If user confirmation = 'Y'

11. Clear screen and display insertion 'form' skeleton
12. Accept contract number
13. Accept model
14. Accept maintenance cost
15. Accept user confirmation
16. Write new data to database
17. Accept repeat response
18. Clear form entries

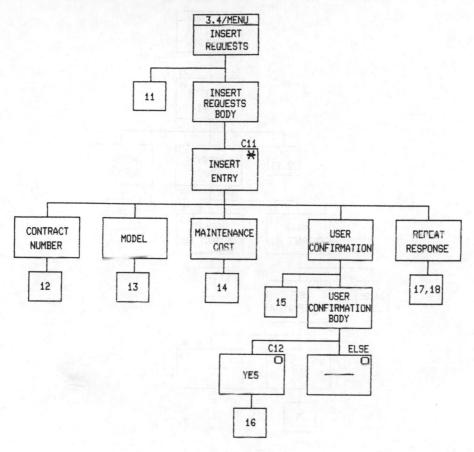

Figure I.2

Next we show the DELETION REQUESTS procedure – see figure I.3.
The operation and condition list is:

C21 – Until user no longer requires this option (note that this is implemented by allocating a QUIT from iteration to the component REPEAT RESPONSE after operation 28)

C22 – If contract number found in database

C23 – If user confirmation = 'Y'

21. Clear screen and display headings with contract no. prompt
22. Accept contract number
23. Attempt to retrieve contract details
24. Display contract details
25. Display prompt and accept user confirmation
26. Delete contract from database

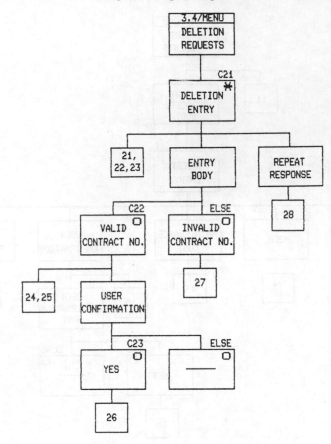

Figure I.3

27. Display error message
28. Display prompt and accept repeat request

Next we show the VIEW REQUESTS procedure — see figure I.4.
The operation and condition list is:

C31 — Until user no longer requires this option (note that this is implemented by
allocating a QUIT from iteration to the component REPEAT RESPONSE
after operation 36)

C32 — If contract number found in database

31. Clear screen and display headings with contract no. prompt
32. Accept contract number
33. Attempt to retrieve contract details
34. Display contract details
35. Display error message
36. Display prompt and accept repeat response

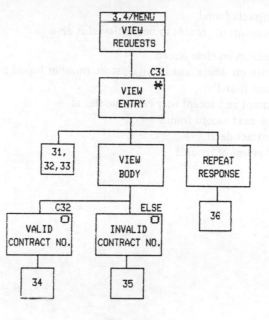

Figure I.4

Next we show the LIST REQUESTS procedure – see figure I.5, and the operation and condition list.

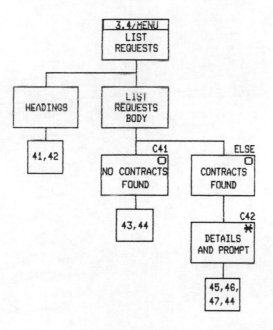

Figure I.5

C41 — If no contracts found
C42 — Until the count of records to be displayed is zero

41. Display headings on clear screen
42. Find all contracts where cost is 'high'; store number found in counter
43. Display 'none found'
44. Display prompt and accept user continue signal
45. Retrieve the next record found
46. Display contract details
47. Decrement count of records

Appendix J: Complete Programs for the Inversion Example (Chapter 9)

```
00100    IDENTIFICATION DIVISION.
00200    **** PROGRAM TO PRODUCE AN INTERMEDIATE FILE ****
00300    **** FROM THE STUDENT FILE                   ****
00400    PROGRAM-ID. STUDRP.
00500    ENVIRONMENT DIVISION.
00600    INPUT-OUTPUT SECTION.
00700    FILE-CONTROL.
00800        SELECT STUDENT-FILE ASSIGN TO DSK.
00900    DATA DIVISION.
01000    FILE SECTION.
01100    FD  STUDENT-FILE
01200        RECORDING MODE IS ASCII
01300        VALUE OF ID "STUDENSEQ".
01400    01 STUDENT-FILE-REC.
01500        03 COURSE-CODE        PIC X(8).
01600        03 NAME               PIC X(20).
01700        03 MARK               PIC 999.
01800    WORKING-STORAGE SECTION.
01900    77   INTER-EOF            PIC 9.
02000    77   COURSE-TOT           PIC S9(5).
02100    77   STORED-COURSE        PIC X(8).
02200    01   DETAIL-RECORD.
02300        03 D-REC-TYPE         PIC X.
02400        03 D-REC-DATA.
02500            05 D-COURSE        PIC X(10).
02600            05 D-NAME          PIC X(22).
02700            05 D-MARK          PIC -(5)9.
02800    01   TOTAL-RECORD.
02900        03 T-REC-TYPE         PIC X.
03000        03 T-REC-DATA.
03100            05 T-COURSE        PIC X(10).
03200            05 FILLER          PIC X(22) VALUE "TOTAL".
03300            05 T-TOTAL         PIC -(5)9.
03400    01   NULL-RECORD          PIC X(40) VALUE LOW-VALUES.
03500    PROCEDURE DIVISION.
03600    PROD-INTER-FILE-SEQ.
03700        OPEN INPUT STUDENT-FILE.
03800        MOVE 0 TO INTER-EOF.
03900        READ STUDENT-FILE
04000            AT END MOVE HIGH-VALUES TO COURSE-CODE.
04100    PROGRAM-BODY-ITER.
04200        IF COURSE-CODE = HIGH-VALUES
04300            GO TO PROGRAM-BODY-END.
04400    COURSE-SEQ.
04500        MOVE 0 TO COURSE-TOT.
04600        MOVE COURSE-CODE TO STORED-COURSE.
04700    COURSE-BODY-ITER.
04800        IF (STORED-COURSE NOT = COURSE-CODE) OR
04900           (COURSE-CODE = HIGH-VALUES)
05000            GO TO COURSE-BODY-END.
```

```
05100      MARK-TO-LINE.
05200          MOVE "D" TO D-REC-TYPE
05300          MOVE COURSE-CODE TO D-COURSE.
05400          MOVE NAME TO D-NAME.
05500          MOVE MARK TO D-MARK.
05600          CALL REP-SR USING INTER-EOF DETAIL-RECORD.
05700          ADD MARK TO COURSE-TOT.
05800          READ STUDENT-FILE
05900              AT END MOVE HIGH-VALUES TO COURSE-CODE.
06000      MARK-TO-LINE-END.
06100          GO TO COURSE-BODY-ITER.
06200      COURSE-BODY-END.
06300      COURSE-TOTAL.
06400          MOVE "T" TO T-REC-TYPE.
06500          MOVE STORED-COURSE TO T-COURSE.
06600          MOVE COURSE-TOT TO T-TOTAL.
06700          CALL REP-SR USING INTER-EOF TOTAL-RECORD.
06800      COURSE-TOTAL-END.
06900      COURSE-END.
07000          GO TO PROGRAM-BODY-ITER.
07100      PROGRAM-BODY-END.
07200          CLOSE STUDENT-FILE.
07300          MOVE 1 TO INTER-EOF.
07400          CALL REP-SR USING INTER-EOF NULL-RECORD.
07500          STOP RUN.
07600      PROD-INTER-FILE-END.
00100      IDENTIFICATION DIVISION.
00200      **** SUBPROGRAM TO PRODUCE REPORT ****
00300      **** FROM INTERMEDIATE FILE      ****
00400      PROGRAM-ID. REP-SR.
00500      ENVIRONMENT DIVISION.
00600      CONFIGURATION SECTION.
00700      SPECIAL-NAMES. CHANNEL (1) IS HEAD-OF-FORM.
00800      INPUT-OUTPUT SECTION.
00900      FILE-CONTROL.
01000          SELECT MARKS-FILE ASSIGN TO DSK.
01100      DATA DIVISION.
01200      FILE SECTION.
01300      FD  MARKS-FILE
01400          RECORDING MODE IS ASCII
01500          VALUE OF ID "MARKS SEQ".
01600      01 MARKS-FILE-REC     PIC X(80).
01700      LINKAGE SECTION.
01800      01 DATA-RECORD.
01900          03 L-REC-TYPE        PIC X.
02000          03 L-REC-DATA        PIC X(38).
02100      77 INTER-EOF          PIC 9.
02200      WORKING-STORAGE SECTION.
02300      77 ENTRY-STATUS        PIC 9  VALUE 1.
02400      77 LINE-COUNT          PIC 99.
02500      01 HEADINGS-REC        PIC X(40) VALUE
02600          "STUDENT MARKS FOR ALL FULL-TIME COURSES".
02700      PROCEDURE DIVISION USING INTER-EOF DATA-RECORD.
02800      PROD-REPORT-SEQ.
02900          GO TO ENTRY-1 ENTRY-2 DEPENDING ON ENTRY-STATUS.
03000      ENTRY-1.
03100          OPEN OUTPUT MARKS-FILE.
03200      PROGRAM-BODY-ITER.
03300          IF INTER-EOF = 1
03400              GO TO PROGRAM-BODY-END.
03500      PAGE-SEQ.
03600      PAGE-HEADING.
03700          WRITE MARKS-FILE-REC FROM HEADINGS-REC
03800                  AFTER HEAD-OF-FORM.
03900          WRITE MARKS-FILE-REC FROM SPACES AFTER 2.
```

```
04000          MOVE 0 TO LINE-COUNT.
04100      PAGE-HEADING-END.
04200      PAGE-BODY-ITER.
04300          IF INTER-EOF = 1 OR LINE-COUNT > 20
04400              GO TO PAGE-BODY-END.
04500      LINE-SEQ.
04600      LINE-BODY-SEL.
04700          IF L-REC-TYPE = "D"
04800              NEXT SENTENCE
04900          ELSE
05000              GO TO LINE-BODY-ELSE-1.
05100      DETAIL.
05200          WRITE MARKS-FILE-REC FROM L-REC-DATA AFTER 1.
05300          ADD 1 TO LINE-COUNT.
05400      DETAIL-END.
05500          GO TO LINE-BODY-END.
05600      LINE-BODY-ELSE-1.
05700      TOTAL.
05800          WRITE MARKS-FILE-REC FROM L-REC-DATA AFTER 2.
05900          WRITE MARKS-FILE-REC FROM SPACES AFTER 2.
06000          ADD 4 TO LINE-COUNT.
06100      TOTAL-END.
06200      LINE-BODY-END.
06300          MOVE 2 TO ENTRY-STATUS.
06400          EXIT PROGRAM.
06500      ENTRY-2.
06600      LINE-END.
06700          GO TO PAGE-BODY-ITER.
06800      PAGE-BODY-END.
06900      PAGE-END.
07000          GO TO PROGRAM-BODY-ITER.
07100      PROGRAM-BODY-END.
07200          CLOSE MARKS-FILE.
07300          EXIT PROGRAM.
07400      PROD-REPORT-END.
```

Figure J.1

```
00100     PROGRAM MARKS (STUDENTFILE,REPORTFILE) ;
00200
00300     TYPE
00400       COURSESTRING   = PACKED ARRAY [1..8] OF CHAR ;
00500       STUDENTRECTYPE =
00600         RECORD
00700           COURSECODE  : COURSESTRING ;
00800           NAME        : PACKED ARRAY [1..20] OF CHAR ;
00900           MARK        : 0..100 ;
01000         END ;
01100
01200     VAR
01300       ENTRYSTATUS    : 1..2 ;
01400       INTEREOF       : BOOLEAN ;
01500       LINECOUNT      : INTEGER ;
01600       STOREDCOURSE   : COURSESTRING ;
01700       COURSETOTAL    : INTEGER ;
01800       RECTYPE        : CHAR ;
01900       STUDENTREC     : STUDENTRECTYPE ;
02000       STUDENTFILE    : FILE OF STUDENTRECTYPE ;
02100       REPORTFILE     : TEXT ;
02200
02300     PROCEDURE REPORTSR ;
02400
02500     LABEL
02600       10,20,9999 ;
02700
02800     CONST
02900       PAGEHDNGS = 'STUDENT MARKS FOR ALL FULL-TIME COURSES'
03000
03100     (* produce report from intermediate file seq *)
03200     BEGIN
03300       IF ENTRYSTATUS = 1 THEN GOTO 10
03400       ELSE IF ENTRYSTATUS = 2 THEN GOTO 20 ;
03500       10:
03600       REWRITE (REPORTFILE) ;
03700       (* program body iter *)
03800       WHILE NOT INTEREOF DO
03900       BEGIN
04000         (* page seq *)
04100           (* page heading *)
04200             PAGE (REPORTFILE) ;
04300             WRITELN (REPORTFILE,PAGEHDNGS:39) ;
04400             WRITELN (REPORTFILE) ;
04500             WRITELN (REPORTFILE) ;
04600             LINECOUNT := 0 ;
04700           (* page heading end *)
04800           (* page body iter *)
04900           WHILE NOT (INTEREOF OR (LINECOUNT > 20)) DO
05000           BEGIN
05100             (* line seq *)
05200               (* line body sel *)
05300               IF RECTYPE = 'D' THEN
05400               BEGIN
05500                 (* detail *)
05600                   WRITELN (REPORTFILE,STUDENTREC.COURSECODE:10,
05700                           STUDENTREC.NAME:22,
05800                           STUDENTREC.MARK:6) ;
05900                 LINECOUNT := LINECOUNT + 1 ;
06000                 (* detail end *)
06100               END
06200               (* line body else 1 *)
06300               ELSE
```

```
06400                    BEGIN
06500                     (* total *)
06600                       WRITELN (REPORTFILE) ;
06700                       WRITELN (REPORTFILE,STOREDCOURSE:10,
06800                               'TOTAL':22,COURSETOTAL:6) ;
06900                       WRITELN (REPORTFILE) ;
07000                       WRITELN (REPORTFILE) ;
07100                       LINECOUNT := LINECOUNT + 4 ;
07200                     (* total end *)
07300                    END ;
07400                   (* line body end *)
07500                   ENTRYSTATUS := 2 ;
07600                   GOTO 9999 ;
07700                   20:
07800                 (* line end *)
07900              END ;
08000            (* page body end *)
08100         (* page end *)
08200      END ;
08300      (* program body end *)
08400      9999:
08500  END ;
08600  (* produce report from intermediate file end *)
08700
08800  (* produce intermediate file from student file seq *)
08900  BEGIN
09000     ENTRYSTATUS := 1 ;
09100     RESET (STUDENTFILE) ;
09200     INTEREOF := FALSE ;
09300     READ (STUDENTFILE,STUDENTREC) ;
09400     WITH STUDENTREC DO
09500     (* program body iter *)
09600     WHILE NOT (COURSECODE = 'ZZZZ    ') DO
09700     BEGIN
09800        (* course seq *)
09900        COURSETOTAL := 0 ;
10000        STOREDCOURSE := COURSECODE ;
10100        (* course body iter *)
10200        WHILE NOT ((STOREDCOURSE <> COURSECODE)
10300                   OR ((COURSECODE = 'ZZZZ    ')) DO
10400        BEGIN
10500           (* mark to line *)
10600              RECTYPE := 'D' ;
10700              REPORTSR ;
10800              COURSETOTAL := COURSETOTAL + MARK ;
10900              READ (STUDENTFILE,STUDENTREC) ;
11000           (* mark to line end *)
11100        END ;
11200        (* course body end *)
11300        (* course total *)
11400           RECTYPE := 'T' ;
11500           REPORTSR ;
11600        (* course total end *)
11700      (* course end *)
11800     END ;
11900     (* program body end *)
12000     INTEREOF := TRUE ;
12100     REPORTSR ;
12200  END.
12300  (* produce intermediate file from student file end *)
```

Figure J.2

```
00100   REM ** produce intermediate file from student file seq **
00110     OPEN "STUDEN.SEQ" FOR INPUT AS FILE #1
00120     ES% = 1
00130     INTER = 0
00140     INPUT #1,COURSE$,STUDENT$,MARK%
00150     REM ** program body iter **
00160       REM end of file is ZZZZ in course
00170       IF COURSE$ = "ZZZZ" GOTO 370
00180       REM ** course seq **
00190         TOTAL% = 0
00200         STOREDCOURSE$ = COURSE$
00210         REM ** course body iter **
00220         IF COURSE$ = "ZZZZ" OR STOREDCOURSE$ <> COURSE$ GOTO 300
00230           REM ** mark to line **
00240             PA$ = "D"
00250             GOSUB 440
00260             TOTAL% = TOTAL% + MARK%
00270             INPUT #1,COURSE$,STUDENT$,MARK%
00280           REM ** mark to line end **
00290         GOTO 210
00300         REM ** course body end **
00310         REM ** course total **
00320           PA$ = "T"
00330           GOSUB 440
00340         REM ** course total end **
00350       REM ** course end **
00360       GOTO 150
00370     REM ** program body end **
00380     CLOSE #1
00390     INTER = 1
00400     GOSUB 440
00410     STOP
00420   REM ** produce intermediate file from student file end **
00430   REM ******************
00440   REM ** produce report from intermediate file seq **
00450     IF ES% = 1 THEN 470
00460     IF ES% = 2 THEN 780
00470     OPEN "MARKS.OUT" FOR OUTPUT AS FILE #2
00480     REM ** program body iter **
00490     IF INTER = 1 GOTO 840
00500       REM ** page seq **
00510         REM ** page heading **
00520           PRINT #2
00530           PRINT #2,"STUDENT MARKS FOR ALL FULL-TIME STUDENTS"
00540           PRINT #2
00550           LINECOUNT% = 0
00560         REM ** page heading end **
00570         REM ** page body iter **
00580           IF LINECOUNT% > 20 OR INTER = 1 GOTO 810
00590           REM ** line seq **
00600             REM ** line body sel **
00610               IF NOT (PA$ = "D") GOTO 670
00620               REM ** detail **
00630                 PRINT #2,COURSE$;TAB(11);STUDENT$;TAB(33);MARK%
00640                 LINECOUNT% = LINECOUNT% + 1
00650               REM ** detail end **
00660               GOTO 750
00670             REM ** line body else 1 **
00680               REM ** total **
00690                 PRINT #2
00700                 PRINT #2,STOREDCOURSE$;TAB(11);" TOTAL";
00705                 PRINT #2,TAB(33);TOTAL%
00710                 PRINT #2
00720                 PRINT #2
```

```
00730                    LINECOUNT%  = LINECOUNT% + 4
00740                  REM ** total end **
00750                  REM ** line body end **
00760                  ES% = 2
00770                  RETURN
00780                  REM entry point 2
00790                REM ** line end **
00800                GOTO 570
00810              REM ** page body end **
00820            REM ** page end **
00830            GOTO 480
00840          REM ** program body end **
00850          CLOSE #2
00860          RETURN
00870      REM ** produce report from intermediate file end **
```

Figure J.3